The

ALCHEMY *of*

YOUR DREAMS

The
ALCHEMY *of*
YOUR DREAMS

A Modern Guide *to the*
Ancient Art *of* Lucid Dreaming
and Interpretation

ATHENA LAZ

A TARCHERPERIGEE BOOK

tarcherperigee

an imprint of Penguin Random House LLC
penguinrandomhouse.com

Most TarcherPerigee books are available at special quantity discounts for bulk purchase for sales promotions, premiums, fund-raising, and educational needs. Special books or book excerpts also can be created to fit specific needs. For details, write: SpecialMarkets@ penguinrandomhouse.com.

Library of Congress Cataloging-in-Publication Data

Names: Laz, Athena, author.
Title: The alchemy of your dreams: a modern guide to the ancient art of
lucid dreaming and interpretation / Athena Laz.
Description: New York: TarcherPerigee,
Penguin Random House LLC, 2021. | Includes index.
Identifiers: LCCN 2020057489 (print) | LCCN 2020057490 (ebook) |
ISBN 9780593327791 (paperback) | ISBN 9780593327807 (ebook)
Subjects: LCSH: Dreams. | Dream interpretation.
Classification: LCC BF1078 .L399 2021 (print) |
LCC BF1078 (ebook) | DDC 154.6/3—dc23
LC record available at https://lccn.loc.gov/2020057489
LC ebook record available at https://lccn.loc.gov/2020057490
p.   cm.

Printed in the United States of America
1st Printing

Book design by Lorie Pagnozzi

For Jed

TABLE OF CONTENTS

I SLEEP SO THAT I MAY SEE

With no memory of how she arrived at this place or point in time, she is aware only that she is standing barefoot on a gravel road. The darkness around her is reverberating with a seeming cacophony of silence and whispers like only the night can make. She surveys the land in an attempt to gather her bearings and as she does the reality sinks in. She's all alone in this place . . . *this place*.

Where is this place, again?

The granular nature of the gravel beneath her cold bare feet distracts her from her thoughts. She looks down bearing witness to her feet—meek and exposed—and, squinting, she sees that she is standing on an "X," marked in red paint.

Curious, she thinks.

In the cold, wet darkness a warm thought appears. She realizes that she can see clearly in the night. In fact, she's always been able to see in the dark. Another trigger of recognition: she's always had the power of choice. With that illumination she now understands that she is currently facing a choice. Stand still and stagnate or move forward boldly into the unknown.

Suddenly her slumber recedes, waking her to the reality of her bed and the room around her. That is life as usual. Yet, with one subtle difference: now, she carries something precious with her. A gift brought back from the dream:

X marks the spot

X is where the treasure lies

X is this red-hot minute

THE TREASURE TROVE THAT IS YOUR DREAMS

All of your dreams are a gift. Yes, even the dreams that scare the life out of (or rather into) you. They are the treasures offered up from within your own psyche and spirit. As renowned writer and analyst Marie-Louise Von Franz proclaimed: dreams don't "waste much spit telling you what you already know." And as I like to drive home, dreams tell you *what you need to know.*

They are the "X" that marks the spot.

By their very nature dreams speak to something much larger, and far more numinous, than what we already know. They speak to all that we don't know. All that we refuse to see. Or simply can't see. All that we wish to see. They speak to the interconnection of all life and our very place within it.

Dreams lift our gaze to show us the multitude of infinite possibilities, and as you will come to discover over the course of this book, when you dream you are guided by something much larger than just your own mind. You are led by spirit in tandem with your psyche. As a result you can receive wisdom, creative inspiration, and powerful solutions that can and will elevate you, should you choose to act on your dream guidance.

This is what "acted on" dreams look like in the world: Larry Page received the idea for Google through a dream; Mary Shelley, the author of *Frankenstein*, used her dreams as inspiration—as does Stephen King; Paul McCartney heard the melody for "Yesterday" in a dream; August Kekulé discovered the ring-like structure of benzene after dreaming of a snake eating its own tail (the ouroboros symbol). Even Niels Bohr dreamed of the structure of the atom.

And as any therapist would know, dreams help us on a night-to-night basis, not just with visionary ideas that move the world. They gift fundamental and transformative insights to help us navigate the daily terrain of life, emotions, relationships, and desires. They help us feel better.

Dreams have been scientifically proven to help regulate negative emotion. They can provide a level of closure and healing when grief takes hold of us. Offer answers to problems that seem immovable during waking hours, and even help to resolve inner conflict.

You will discover that all dreams are abundant offerings. Now, this isn't to say that all of your dreams will feel easy—a nocturnal narrative of bliss and pleasure. This is because dreams help to guard against self-deception and in doing so they often pack a metaphoric punch, encouraging you to ask: What is the message I'm not hearing? The "thing" that I'm not seeing? The path I'm afraid to follow? The feeling I'm unwilling to feel?

Answering these questions in waking life requires a depth of honesty and emotional resolve that is often simply easier to ignore. Dreams, however, knock nightly on the psyche, waking us up to our inner truth. A truth that can extend to a life well lived should you, the dreamer, bravely turn to face your insights. You know the "thing," the feelings, the patterns, and the longings that stand between you and your most aligned waking life.

A DOORWAY TO YOUR DREAMSCAPES

This book is intended to be a doorway for you to walk bravely through in order to discover your own dreamscapes. But before you cross the threshold I want to briefly offer my background in order to give you a broad overview of my approach. By profession I am a counseling psychologist, dream expert, and a fourth-generation intuitive. I am also a self-taught and avid lucid dreamer. I have had powerful dreams since I was a child and as I got older my dreams called to me even more.

In fact, one might say that dreams chose me to be a mouthpiece for them, but that's really a story for another time. So for now, let's just say that I chose to specialize in dreamwork because I found dreams to be the most direct path to transformation, growth, and spiritual awakening. Quite simply, because we get out of our own way when we sleep, our dreams can help us enormously.

I have worked with thousands of incredible people worldwide through my courses, monthly membership programs, in-person workshops, and retreats, all of which are aimed at helping people to look to their dreams, psyche, and inner knowing for the answers they seek.

I orient my work toward the ancient meaning of the word "psychotherapy." Etymologically, the word links back to the "psyche" (soul, breath, spirit) and "therapy" (healing, treatment). The root essence of the word reminds us that psychotherapy is about soul healing. In other words, psychotherapy is more than healing just the mind and the emotions. It's about soulful connection and well-being.

I believe that we need to weave the spirit and soul back into contemporary psychological practices in order to have both a more balanced interior and exterior world. In order to truly experience deep, long-lasting, and profound shifts in life we need to work with all aspects of ourselves. That is the mind, body, and spirit.

For this reason I came to the decision to move beyond the scope of modern psychology because I found it too constricting both for myself and for my clients. Nevertheless I am forever grateful for the sound, enriching, and ethical platform psychology gave me and from which a lot of my work springs forth.

Psychology is a strong and essential foundation to build from. It is a vital piece in the puzzle of consciousness and human understanding—as is science, mysticism, and spirituality. I don't believe that pioneer psychologists ever intended for the field of psychology to be the "only answer" or hold "all the answers" for wholehearted living and consciousness. The human experience is as varied as the people living on this planet and to believe that just one method or school of thought is the right one is, in my opinion, simply stifling.

Because you're reading this book, I'd bet that you are interested in a broader realm of what it means to be alive and to explore whatever brings existential meaning to your life. I'm going to dip and dive around many schools of thought, pulling out the ones that have felt most accurate and helpful to me, sharing them here with you in the hope that they will be equally helpful to you.

Lastly, as we all are subjective beings, I've tried to make the practical exercises in this book as helpful and varied as possible. I've done this in order to offer you a higher chance of experiencing all the different facets of dreaming for yourself. That said, this is *your* journey. If something doesn't resonate with you, please feel free to move on to another exercise to find the ones that work best for you! Let's begin.

THE DREAM SPECTRUM

I believe that we reconnect with a greater unified consciousness (the Universe, spirit, source) every night when we sleep.

To clarify, I use the words "Spirit," "Universe," or "Non-Physical" interchangeably to mean the life force of all things. You may recognize this force as God, energy, source, or simply as a stream of consciousness. Please feel free to choose and use whichever word or statement that you feel most comfortable with throughout the course of this book.

The belief that when we fall asleep we reconnect with a spiritual source is not uniquely mine. Hinduism, Judaism, Christianity, Buddhism, and Shintoism, to name just a few spiritual schools of thought, speak to this idea. And so nightly we are gifted with the ability to garner a greater perspective, while at the same time gaining an increase in physical well-being through restorative sleep.

This greater perspective gives rise to many different kinds of dreams. We can experience regular dreams; warning dreams; precognitive or prophetic dreams; collective dreams; and lucid dreams. You will discover all of these dreams over the course of this book. That said, it's helpful to differentiate between what regular dreams and lucid dreams are right from the start.

Regular or "normal" dreams are rich with imagery, symbols, and stories. These dreams are the nightly excursions that you generally find yourself taking. At times these dreams are bright and vivid. Much like the dream-story I shared with you at the beginning of this book. Other times they are completely forgettable. Perhaps, like the dream you had last Wednesday?

Over the course of this book I've used the term "regular" and "normal" to describe these kinds of dreams. This is simply for ease of reading and clarification. From the outset I want you to know that these everyday dreams are anything but mundane or regular. I'll even venture to say that dreams may be our greatest spiritual teachers, yet the most often dismissed in the morning light.

Regular dreams make up the bulk of your life, and as you journey through this book you will come to discover just how generous these dreams are. How they always guide you.

Filled with familiar and unfamiliar people, places, events, and characters, these dreams speak to you symbolically and metaphorically. In chapter three, you will discover the depth of insight available to you via this symbolic form of dream interpretation. In doing the practice you will also come to learn exactly how to decode your soulful dream messages for greater personal well-being and growth.

Now, I'd like you to muse over this little something: Have you ever had a dream in which you realized you were dreaming?

If yes, then you went from a regular dream to a lucid dream! You traveled up the dream spectrum, so to speak. If your answered no, then get excited because your dream exploration is about to become more masterful with every page of this book!

For clarity: regular dreams are dreams in which you have no idea you are dreaming. It's only when you wake up in the morning that you realize that you were in fact dreaming. In stark contrast, lucid dreams are dreams in which you are actively aware that you are dreaming *while you are actually in the dream.*

In other words, you find yourself "awake" in a dream even though physiologically your body is still asleep. You can then go on to explore your dream with cognitive awareness and intent of will, altering the dreamscape as you like, something you cannot do in a regular dream.

Let's return to the regular dream story that I shared with you at the beginning of this book for greater depth of clarity:

A woman suddenly finds herself standing barefoot on a cold gravel road. She's disorientated. She scans the horizon in order to grasp where she is. A realization strikes her: she is alone, all alone in this strange place. And in that moment, she has a very illuminating thought. She asks herself: Where is this place?

That self-reflective question could have "woken her up" to the fact that she was in a dream! *That she was dreaming.* But in the dream, her cold feet distract her, and so she forgets about her probing question, resulting in the dream simply playing out, that is, without her conscious awareness.

Had the dream been a lucid one, the experience could have played out as follows:

A woman suddenly finds herself standing barefoot on a cold gravel road. She's disorientated. She scans the horizon in order to grasp where she is. She realizes that she is all alone in this strange place. And in that moment, she has a very illuminating thought. She asks herself: Where is this place?

That thought then leads to an "aha" moment because she continues to question herself: "I've never been to this place. How did I get here? Where was I before this?"

And with these self-reflective questions a memory (and answer!) rises to the forefront of her consciousness: the last thing you did was get into bed. This groundbreaking answer leads her to think: "I have to be dreaming. This is a dream. *I'm dreaming.*"

Therein lies the fundamental difference between a lucid dream and a regular dream. In a lucid dream you are awake in the dream. In a regular dream, you dream because you are asleep.

Now, you may be thinking, has lucid dreaming been proven to be real? And the answer is a resounding yes! Lucid dreaming was scientifically confirmed in the West in 1975 when two researchers, Hearne and Worsley, did a set of dream experiments in their lab that proved it. Since then, a growing body of scientific and academic research has emerged, aimed at demystifying the practice of lucid dreams.

Prior to this scientific evidence hitting Western shores, lucid dreaming was (and still is) a revered practice in many faiths and beliefs such as Buddhism, Hinduism, and shamanism. In fact, it is an ancient dream practice that spans millennia. People have been lucid dreaming for centuries, and Western science has by comparison only recently joined in on the conversation.

At this point, I am often asked: How does lucid dreaming help? And more important, how can it help me? This book is in many ways dedicated to answering that question.

Pragmatically speaking, lucid dreaming can help you to transform stuck emotion, help you to physically heal, and aid in proficiency of developing a skill (like playing music or meditating), among myriad other benefits. You can also develop meta-compassion through lucid dreaming, receive spiritual teachings, and even prepare for the moments after death. Yet, Tibetan Bön Buddhist Tenzin Wangyal Rinpoche's words gracefully offer a golden snippet of the penultimate benefit:

> *The first step in the dream practice is quite simple: one must recognize the great potential that dream holds for the spiritual journey. Normally, the dream is thought to be "unreal," as opposed to "real" waking life. But there is nothing more real than the dream.*

Lucid dreaming is about so much more than just controlling your actions in your dreams and surface-level benefits. It's about connecting with the source of who you really are. It's about the dance between the seen and the unseen, the waking world and the dream world, and you as the bridge between the two.

Through all of your dreams you will come to rediscover the gifts already held in the depths of your inner being. You will come to realize that you are actively creating your life. That you are the dreamer of both your dream and your waking life.

Every night, you are able to move between waking consciousness and sleep consciousness through the vehicle of regular dreaming.

That in itself is pretty incredible.

Add lucid dreaming to the mix and you are on the brink of something downright magical: the ability to be aware (and move through) both forms of consciousness or "reality."

We've all had dreams that felt so real, so vivid, that at the time, for all you knew, they were real. It's only on waking that you realized that you were in a dream state. Yet, with lucid dreaming you actually know that you are exploring consciousness.

Experiencing lucid dreaming brings you to a broader existential question: If you have awareness of two forms of consciousness, then what is this third form of awareness (or meta-awareness)? This is a question I hope that you will explore of your own accord once you become the deliberate traveler of your dreamscape.

I believe that all of our dreams are here to show us infinite possibilities, highlighting the vibration (both individually and collectively) that we are both projecting outward and calling in, ultimately offering us an opportunity to shift our alignment as needed. In other words, our dreams can help us to sort out how we feel; to recognize what energy we are putting out into the world and to course correct if and as needed; to potentially see what may come to pass; and to reconnect with spirit on a nightly basis.

SLEEP WELL KNOWING
THAT EVERYTHING HAS ITS VALUE

Whichever dream brought you here—the regular dream, the precognitive dream, the warning dream, the symbolic dream, or the lucid dream—it is simply my wish that by the time you come to the end of this book you will become a deliberate dreamer.

So whether you are or are not ever able to lucid dream, please know that all of your dreams are important, offering you ridiculously rich insights. If you try to put your dreams on a hierarchy of better or more valuable experiences, you may miss the everyday magic that happens during your regular dreaming. And although this book will teach you exactly how to lucid dream, its main purpose is to awaken a deep love of dreaming within you. So that you can experience the phenomena that are all dreams.

It's important in dream work to first understand regular (symbolic) dreaming so that you have a strong foundation to work off of. Regular dream work lends itself to the process of lucid dreaming. You will discover exactly how your emotions, thoughts, and beliefs influence all of your dreams, which is a crucial understanding needed to participate in lucid dreaming.

Ultimately, dreaming is a joyful path. One in which you will discover that there is no right or wrong way of journeying down that path. That said, in order to awaken this deep love of dreaming, you actually have to be able to remember your dreams on waking. Here's how:

Before you fall asleep it is helpful to set the intention that you are going to recall your dreams on waking. If you commit to doing this every night, you should begin to see that your dream recall will increase.

An intention is simply a heartfelt thought that you put a lot of consideration and energy into. It is a whispered declaration that you put out to the Universe. Intentions are also psychologically significant because you are committing to whatever it is that you are intending to do on a psyche level too.

Your intention could be a hope that you have for your dream practice or simply for your life. Once you've set your intention, close your eyes. Then take a few deep, nourishing breaths and say the following words before you go to sleep:

"It is safe for me to explore the world of my dreams tonight. I will have good dreams and remember them in the morning. I am ready to explore all facets of my dream life. I am fully willing to allow my dream guidance to assist me."

On waking, try and not move your body at all, simply remain as still as you can—this usually takes a bit of practice! Keep your eyes closed, and while you are lying there, still, you should try to replay your dream in your mind. This is so that your brain (more specifically the hippocampus) can catch up and store your dream to memory. Once you feel like you have a firm grip on it, then note your dream down in a journal.

Here's how to dream journal:

Keep a notebook next to your bed, and on waking, write down exactly what you remember about your dream. Include as much information as possible: note any scenery, people, feelings, and dream figures that featured in your dream. It can also be helpful to underline anything that feels particularly important to you at the time. Note your dreams down in the most detailed way that you can, and attempt to recall anything and everything from the dream, even if seemingly insignificant.

Details help because you are really creating a collection of your dream symbols through documenting your dreams. Later on, I'm also going to show you how you can decode your dream symbols, so if you begin now, you should have enough material to interpret some of your dreams by the time you reach that specific chapter.

A symbol that may seem unimportant upon first reflection may, in the long term, turn out to be significant. For example, you may not realize that the sun is always present in your dreams. Or perhaps the opposite is true: the sun is never present. The sun is a symbol that could quite easily be forgotten or disregarded, but there it is, illuminating your dreams nightly. It may be showing you how to connect to the visible essence that sustains life and that which is also symbolic of your inner light.

Ready?

CHAPTER 1

WHAT'S YOUR WHY?

A vast expanse of burned orange sand stretches before me as far as the eye can see. Rolling one upon another, the dunes create a never-ending vista mimicking water but made of earth. Each grain whispers a tale of time long forgotten, waiting to be heard. I stand mesmerized, breathing in the silence and beauty before me. The wind blows gently and I sway with it rhythmically. Fully immersed in the vast openness, I begin to remember that I've been to this very place before.

Slowly I move my hands through the sand. Pulling up a weighty handful of desert earth, I look down to see that the sand is glimmering. The colors change with every fractal of light as I pour the sand from one hand to the other. Focusing on the sensation of the granules against my hands, time feels still.

Both my hands are now open and the sand slips through my fingers. As each grain passes, I unburden myself from the heaviness of my history. I feel weightless, almost too light, so much so that I try to focus my attention on my bare feet. As I look down at them, they begin to disappear into the sand beneath me. Limb by limb, bone by bone, I am integrated into the desert.

Conscious of this transformation, I realize that I am the whole desert and also just a grain.

I wake up with an overwhelming sense of serenity, only to have it cut short by the alarm going off, grounding me right back into my everyday, human experience. And isn't that just the way? How the mystical is so neatly wrapped up within the mundane. Acting as a sacred reminder that our lives are made of present moments, one following the next, until death transforms us once again.

✳

Before you continue to read on, I'd like you to spend a couple of minutes thinking about why you are motivated to do dream work. Ask yourself: Why do I want to do this? Write your thoughts down on paper without censoring them. Then keep what you've written close so that you can refer to it later. Once you've done that, come back here and carry on reading.

DREAM WORK AND THE PSYCHE

Dreams help us to question and alter our deep-seated beliefs and to take note of what we are creating, and manifesting, in our everyday lives. They serve to help us live a fuller and richer life while also showing us which parts of our psyches are underdeveloped, so that we can work toward greater psychological integration and emotional well-being.

From a psychological and personal-growth perspective, that means working with the collective unconscious, your personal unconscious, emotions, drives, and the equivalent symbolic representations that appear in your dream work. Something I am actively going to show you how to do throughout the course of this book. From a spiritual level that means working in tandem with spirit.

Take my Desert Dream as an example. That dream helped me to more fully discover, and then express, my feelings around death and dying. At the time I was afraid of death on a deep emotional level. More specifically, my fear was about not knowing how it would happen. Up until that dream, I had never really given myself the space or permission to really reflect on why that was the case and how it made me feel.

If someone asked me how I felt about dying, I flippantly laughed it off, saying that "we all gotta do it sometime." Or I redirected the conversation to another topic. In other words, my fears and emotions around mortality really freaked me out, and so to neutralize the anxiety that came up when I thought about it, I portrayed a breezy and light attitude—the opposite of what I was feeling internally.

My behavior in this instance is typical of a psychological defense mechanism known as reaction formation. A defense mechanism is when your mind responds in a specific way to help minimize internal conflict. All of us have defense mechanisms, and learning more fully about them can assist you in your journey of personal growth.

Specifically, reaction formation is when you convert how you really feel by presenting a more personally (or socially) acceptable response in order to lessen internal unease. This doesn't mean that you have accepted how you feel. It means that you defend against it by showing the opposite of what you feel.

Although I reflected a calm exterior when the topic of death came up, my original fear did not disappear. It still existed but was hidden from my conscious awareness via my defense mechanism. In other words, my rejected thoughts and emotions associated with the topic of death persisted, but outside of my awareness. That is, unconsciously. So my dream came to shake me awake. To assist me in facing myself.

Like your dreams do as well.

DREAM CONTENT AND YOUR HIDDEN WHY | DREAMS REVEAL YOUR INTERIOR LIFE

It is helpful to work with dream content. By dream content I mean the images, dream figures, landscapes, and symbols that appear in your dreams. I believe that dream content is influenced by spirit, our vibration, the collective unconscious, and the personal unconscious. I feel it is necessary to have an understanding of these terms (if you don't already) to do great dream work.

Most behavior is heavily influenced by unconscious factors. That is, drives, motives, and impulses that are outside of your active awareness. For example, you may really want to succeed in a health or financial goal but every time you commit to changing, you find yourself self-sabotaging along the way. In an instance like this, it is likely that you are working with a deep-seated belief that is hidden from your awareness, which is getting in the way of what you are trying to create, manifest, and experience in your life.

You may, for example, have a drive to fail because you unconsciously believe that other people will cut you down if you become too "successful," "good-looking," or "visible." (Success can take many shapes and forms; I'm simply highlighting a few common examples for brevity.) Your unconscious belief gets in the way. On the one hand you have a drive to succeed but on the other you are afraid to be successful. In order to mitigate these two diverging drives you self-sabotage by procrastinating, or simply by never taking the right action to get you there.

At the same time, in order to help you become more integrated as a person and to help you create a life that feels good to you, your dreams will offer you images or scenarios to make you aware of these deep-seated and unconscious beliefs.

Your dreams will be in the form of imagery designed specifically to alert you to how you feel on a deep level and what you need to pay attention to in your waking life.

For instance, you may have a dream that you are in an elevator that is taking you to the top floor of a building—only to then have the elevator doors fail to open. Or alternatively, you may dream of being in an elevator that suddenly starts rapidly descending, leaving you feeling afraid and panicked!

Your dream is symbolically telling you that while you are the person in the dream, your beliefs are the elevator. In other words: the elevator doors will automatically open up when you stop and face your own self-sabotaging beliefs. Your dream is alerting you to the need to willingly choose to descend (symbolically: the elevator plummets rapidly toward the lower floors) into the depths of your own psyche.

That is so that you can address any beliefs that are holding you back. If you do so, the doors of opportunity (and the elevator doors) will likely open too. Your dream is guiding you to a sustainable way of moving forward positively through addressing any issues that may be outside of your awareness.

Alternatively, you could have a dream in which you are in a flower shop intending to buy roses but instead you somehow end up with a bunch of tall poppies. You really wanted the roses but instead you are left with a bouquet of poppies. How disappointing!

In the context of the dream, the poppies are symbolically representative of the fear of experiencing "tall poppy syndrome." This is a colloquialism used (commonly in Australia and New Zealand) to describe the desire to insult or cut down people who are highly successful.

The flower imagery here is the message of the dream. It shows you the difference between what you want (the roses) and what you are actually experiencing (the poppies). The fact that you are in control of buying the roses and then something suddenly occurs (outside of your awareness) that leaves you with the poppies, shows you two things:

The first is that you weren't gifted the flowers. You went to purchase them (that is, this dream is about what is in your control). Had someone gifted you the flowers in your dream, then it is more likely that you are dealing with a relationship dynamic.

The second is that the dream imagery shows you that somehow in the act of purchasing the flowers you end up with the poppies, that is, something happened outside of your awareness that resulted in your ending up with a bunch of flowers that you didn't want.

In both of these examples, the dream shows you images that are created to help you uncover your deep-seated unconscious beliefs and fears (and your associated energetic vibration) with the ultimate goal of transforming the belief for the better so that you can manifest and create better.

The dreamer, in this example, could succeed by simply allowing themselves to act more authentically regardless of "what other people think." They could allow themselves to "grow tall" with success regardless of the perceived threat of criticism. They could become the rose.

Most of the time people ascribe these types of limiting deep-seated beliefs to the workings of the subconscious mind. The subconscious mind delineates some form of awareness just beneath the conscious mind. But really when people do this, they are actually referring to (from a psychological perspective) deeper aspects of the unconscious aspects of the mind. I prefer to the use of the word "unconscious" because it more accurately describes what it is.

Equally, a differentiation between the collective and personal unconscious can be made. This is not something that is done in reference to the subconscious mind and why I don't actively use the term throughout the course of this book.

In order to work well with your dream content it's necessary to grasp the difference between your personal unconscious and the collective unconscious. That is because dream content is influenced by both sources. And I believe that each source calls for a slightly different approach to dream interpretation or lucid dream interaction. As you'll soon discover.

Understanding Your Personal Unconscious In Dream Work

Your psyche is the storehouse of all the experiences you've ever had to date. That means all your memories and experiences that you've experienced, for better or worse, are stored within your mind whether you can remember them or not. According to the analytic theory developed by noted psychiatrist Carl Jung, the personal unconscious is the substrata of the psyche that contains these personal memories and experiences.

In other words, your personal unconscious houses any memories that you may have pushed out of your awareness and cannot actively recall. As well as any memories (both pleasant and unpleasant) that you may have simply forgotten over time. When I refer to the personal unconscious I mean to highlight the information that is present within your mind from your lived experience.

Your personal unconscious is also home to any complexes that you may be working with. Very simply, a complex is a collection of thoughts, images, ideas, and memories that are emotionally charged and that come together to form a single theme. For example: love, sex, power. All of us deal with complexes, and for the most part, they only become a serious issue when we flat-out deny their existence.

In your dreams, evidence of any complexes that you may be dealing with will appear through the imagery, scenes, and symbols that you dream about. Let's say that one night you have a dream where you are stuck in a small space. Then, a few nights later, you dream that you are in a car being chased by a person in another car. A week later you dream that you have to make an important call but can't find the phone. And so it goes.

Although all the dream places, figures, and images are different in the three dreams, they all are charged with the same emotion—an overwhelming anxiety. This is reflected by the feelings of tension and worry that run through all three of the dreams. The dreamer is being made aware of how they feel at a core level and the complex that they are dealing with.

A complex points out that we may be in a state of tension. This doesn't mean that anything is wrong. It simply means that we are resisting something, and by doing so, creating inner tension. Dreams then offer us guidance about this tension. They offer us a better way forward. They show us what we are resisting through specific and evocative dream scenarios and imagery, so that we can get the message to alter our vibration and lives accordingly.

When you dream in relation to a complex, your dream attempts to draw your attention to any polarized experiences or concepts that you may be grappling with. Dreaming also raises your awareness of the paradigm of opposites or duality. Once you become aware of these polarized experiences (good/bad, light/dark, sterile/fertile), you can then alter how you feel about and relate to them.

As was the case with my dream of the desert and sand. In that dream, I was shown that I was grappling with two opposites: life and death. A tension that exists at all times. My dream was pivotal in helping me to unify my inner conflict around living and dying. The dream left me with a sense of serenity and peace, the reverse of my emotional and mental fears, showing me that I could accept my feelings around dying to reach a new level of acceptance.

Through that dream I learned that death can be a great motivator and liberator, and that I could live more fully, and authentically, by accepting that death is certain. Death is ever present as long as we are alive. Opposites do not cease to exist, but a third way of living appears through the radical acceptance and containment of the one in relation to the other, and vice versa. As you read these words, you have the ability to hold these opposites in union by bringing your awareness to both.

Through observing dichotomy without running away from it or gravitating to one side, we become more integrated. And in doing so we begin to willingly alter our level of energetic alignment. My dream helped me to become more integrated, and I believe it was a powerful message from spirit showing me that I was ready to transform my way of living.

I strongly feel that we never see anything that we are spiritually un-prepared to see—although psychologically it may not always feel this way. You are aware of what you dream for a reason. No matter what you discover, just know that the information presented in your dreams will be helpful if you chose to act on their guidance.

When you reach the chapter on decoding your dream messages you will see just how your personal unconscious, and any associated com-plexes, interact with you on a nightly basis. That is in relation to the symbols and images that you dream of. So again, if you aren't already dream journaling, then let this be your motivation to get started!

Working with the dream material helps because we don't just dream of issues and complexes. We dream of soulful solutions and guidance as to what next step to take. We are being guided through the medium of our dreams to understand our hearts and minds.

When you choose to actively work with your unconscious content, life gets interesting because you are participating in the journey toward discovering your true Self. A lifelong journey that actively allows you to change what you need to, in order to feel better and create better.

Understanding the Collective Unconscious in Dream Work

The collective unconscious is another concept that was created by Carl Jung. In its most simple explanation, the collective unconscious is all the inherited information that we, as humans, are born with. The collective unconscious is not your personal unconscious. It is the storehouse of all human experience.

In spiritual lingo the collective unconscious can be seen as our ability to access, and be influenced by, universal wisdom.

We begin to understand the collective unconscious clearly when we look at the mythology, rituals, and stories (and the associated symbols) of ancient civilizations. It is clear that early civilizations pulled from a shared unconscious in their attempt to explain their existence and interactions with the world, both physically seen and unseen. It also explains why many cultures have myths and fairy tales that draw parallels globally—despite their being hundreds or thousands of miles apart. For instance, there are many versions of the similar creation myths that span different time periods and cultures.

Ultimately, ancestral wisdom stems from the collective unconscious and is also passed down to us individually through storytelling and learned behavior. Some of these stories, or narratives, are helpful, and others limiting.

For example, a woman may want to be financially successful in her own right but she may stem from a lineage where this is not done. Or where all the women before her have struggled financially due to systemic limits. By virtue of this, she inherits (either implicitly or explicitly) a deep-seated belief that women, in general, cannot create wealth. She herself, being a woman, is now thrown into internal conflict.

She wants to create abundance but she has been taught that it is impossible (or very difficult) to do so by virtue of her being a woman. And so in order to manage these conflicting beliefs she takes on the role of a "princess" in her life. (Her dreams will symbolically mimic or mirror this narrative by displaying symbols of self-victimization. She may even dream of regal and poor dream figures interacting with one another in multiple ways.)

So she morphs herself into a princess who is now in need of rescuing in her waking life and in doing so she finds a rich prince who saves her. (By the way, the prince is likely also playing out an inherited role and can equally step out of this role should he choose to.)

Her deep-seated beliefs around wealth stem from both the collective unconscious, the active experiences of her personal ancestry, and her life.

At any time, she can summon her inner courage and rescue herself. Up until she saves herself, she will have dreams that call her awareness to these beliefs so that she may change them! Her dreams will metaphorically send nightly reminders for her to claim her inner power. To create wealth so that she can be free.

She may dream that she is being chased by a beast or dark figure so that she can turn to confront it or even slay it. (This dream shows her that she can be the heroine of her own life and conquer her fears.) She may even dream that her hands are broken and that she needs to tend to them. (Her life is in her hands.) Or she may even dream of the women in her lineage being handicapped, bound, or hurt in dream scenarios that mimic her current life experiences. (She dreams of her grandmother hobbling through a visually accurate representation of her current-day work office or home). The dream imagery will be highly evocative and specific in order to get her to own her inner power in her waking life.

Until she faces her own internalized and inherited deep-seated beliefs, she will be held captive by them. This is true for all of us.

The way out of any unhealthy pattern is to face any deep-seated beliefs that we hold around the issue. We can do this through dream work or through any other form of active unconscious work. In doing this kind of healing work we then find ourselves in a position to write a new narrative—one that better suits what we actually want to experience.

Ultimately, you can create (or manifest) what you want more easily and quickly when you become aware of your own inherited, deep-seated beliefs and, more importantly, change how you feel about them. That is because you can step out of resistance and into alignment with what you actually want to create in your own life, not what you have simply been taught to re-create.

Luckily, we all have access to the unconscious through our dreams. In our regular dreams we interact with the unconscious symbolically.

In our lucid dreams we interact with the unconscious with active and direct awareness. I dive into this fundamental difference in the later chapter on dream figures, so for now simply ask yourself:

What is it that I want to experience in my life? More money, ease, love, health, and safety? Whatever it is, you may need to look at the stories and beliefs that you have around what you are trying to attain. You are worthy of receiving good despite any cultural program-ming, intergenerational trauma patterning, or personal experiences that have taught you otherwise. And your dreams will show you how to get there.

When you choose to work with both the collective and personal un-conscious in your life and dreams, you begin to release yourself from the shackles of any long-standing and restrictive beliefs. With that it becomes easier to act on your heart's desires and not your unconscious pulls because you are aware of what they are. In both your everyday dreams and your lucid dreams, you have an opportunity to uncover your underlying motivations—your "why." And as you've seen, know-ing what they are can revolutionize your life for the better!

For example, I worked with a client who *really* wanted to experience lucid dreaming. When I asked him why he wanted to lucid dream, he couldn't tell me. After chatting for a while, it turned out that he wanted to control his dream life because in his waking life he felt extremely helpless and powerless.

He was so set on experiencing the feeling of expansion of lucid dreams.

That is because the exhilaration of feeling free was the exact opposite experience of what he was going through at that particular time in his waking life.

Lucid dreaming became a very helpful way for him to reclaim his ability to respond to situations well, first in his sleep, then in his waking life. It was a positive (and easier) way for him to create dream experiences that felt expansive and to then carry those feelings through to his waking life. In other words, it was a helpful emotional experience for him that led him to take action on the issues that were holding him back.

Through his lucid dreams he discovered that he already had the inner power to meet life with presence, willingness, and purpose. He recognized that he needed to take action and to stop believing in the victim narrative that he was previously telling over and over again in his waking life.

You may find that the reason you want to lucid dream may be equally as insightful and helpful. Or your motivation may be more emotionally light in nature. For example, many people have simply wanted to experience more deliberate, lucid dreams because they've experienced spontaneous ones and know just how amazing they are! No matter your underlying motivation—that is your hidden "why"— your dreams will always guide you forward.

PRACTICAL EXERCISE:
SELF-REFLECTIVE JOURNALING

Earlier in this chapter I asked you to write down what motivated you to begin doing dream work. I'd like you to now go back and read what you wrote with the intention of noticing any beliefs or patterns that may have sprung up. Do you feel like you have unconscious beliefs that are influencing your motivation to do dream work?

Understanding your own motivation to do dream work in all senses is insightful and helpful. You may find that, unlike my Desert Dream, your underlying motivation comes from a place of integration as opposed to a place of avoidance or fear.

No matter what you discover, just know that the information in your dreams will be helpful if you chose to act on their guidance. Ultimately you know yourself best. And you have the inner power to change anything that is no longer serving you well in your life. Dreams strongly guide you back to your inner strength and wisdom.

SELF-REFLECTIVE QUESTIONS:

1. What is currently working well in my life?

2. What isn't working so well in my life?

3. Are the issues that you listed above one-off problems or are these long-standing patterns of difficulty that you've struggled with your whole life? For example: Has money always been an issue? Or the inability to find a loving partner?

4. If you answered yes to the questions above, then it's likely that you are dealing with an unconscious set of beliefs. If so, are you ready to let your dreams, both lucid and normal, show you how to move positively forward in your life?

5. Do you feel like you are playing out an assigned role or pattern in your life? Are you always the victim, the nurturer, the protector, or the provider?

CHAPTER 2

EMOTIONS, INSTINCTS, AND ALL OF YOUR DREAMS

Many of us have been there. When we arrive at a moment and can't believe that this, *this* is how "we," "it," or "things" turned out. There are so many reasons why this happens and none of them are to be condemned. Perhaps your relationship or marriage didn't end up the way you imagined it would. Maybe you were so steadily robbed of something deeply sacred to you that shutting down felt like it was the only option. Perhaps you were well tamed as a child, so much so that politeness became a cage you rattle in as an adult.

Maybe you unknowingly morphed yourself into the image of the perfect parent, lover, child, or boss and now that is all that others, including you, can see.

Perchance you followed a path, even though deep down you knew better, that left you high and dry. Or just maybe you obsessively chased a shiny goal, only to reach it and realize that it wasn't worth the heavy price you paid along the way.

What I hear most often in response to this isn't *why did this happen*, as you would maybe imagine. But rather, and usually far more distressingly, when—*when did this happen?*

We can lose the connection to our instinctual life very easily if we are not careful. The instinctive nature is the undomesticated part of us that intuitively and deeply knows how to navigate life's terrain and cycles. Either due to societal or cultural pressures, trauma, or self-inflicted choices we become disconnected from our own instincts and emotions.

Sometimes the loss is a slow burn. Like when you become a parent, or a CEO, and then suddenly one morning, a few years in, you realize that you're unhappy. You've back-burnered your needs, not just the basic ones but more importantly the deeper instinctive needs that leave you feeling fulfilled. You martyred your well-being for something or someone.

Other times the instinctive nature is lost the moment an agreement is made.

I see this most often with people who are in *loveless* marriages.

Where all of their financial needs are taken care of but at the high cost of having to be the gilded significant other. Or when a person experiences a trauma so cutting that their connection to their own instinctive nature is damaged as a direct result.

Luckily, the instinctive nature is not concerned with what has or has not happened. It is only concerned with where you are right now and whether you will willingly reconnect with it. The instinctive nature doesn't care if you are the perfect parent, partner, lover, or boss. And it most certainly does not care about how much money you have. The instinctive nature is only concerned with how well you dance with your life. It is waiting for you to ask:

Am I both nourished *and alive?*

The dream life becomes highly provocative when we lose touch with our instinctive nature. This is the psyche's counterbalance measure to rectify well-being. And I mean psyche here in its original sense, meaning Soul.

Your soul will call to you to restore your creative life instincts before you permanently become part of the living dead. It will speak loudly and clearly to rescue you from your numbness. Take the following example of how the psyche can beckon us through our dreams:

A stay-at-home mom had become a carcass of a woman sleepwalking through her life. In her words, she relayed to me that she had fallen into an abyss and no longer cared. She told me (and reassured herself) that she was happily married and that nothing was "really wrong."

Her children were happy. Her partner loved her. They had their health.

So she simply got up in the morning and did *"what she had to do"*! But the abyss was still there, and her life? Well, she humdrummed along, feeling absolutely nothing. Numb as ice. One night she had a dream so powerful that it forced her to pay attention, and on waking she just had to discover its meaning. Her dream goes as follows:

Abby* is at her local gym. She walks through the gym much like she does her waking life, robotically, routinely, and with a lackluster attitude. She gets through the gym check-in area with a quick nod and then she starts to head toward the pool.

As she continues to walk forward she suddenly notices that her towel is beginning to pop out of her gym bag. This frustrates her. Continuing to move forward but slowing her pace, she tries to shove her towel back into the bulging bag. As she pushes the towel deeper into the bag, other items then begin to pop out. Ugh! Now, with laser focus she forcefully shoves everything down into the bag.

After quite a bit of resistance everything miraculously manages to fit into the overstuffed bag. Now, with all of this happening, she only just realizes that she has reached the top of the stairs that lead down to the pool.

She mentally acknowledges the stairs and then begins to carefully

---

* Here, and in the examples that follow, an asterisk indicates a fictitious name is used.

step down onto each step. As she goes down, step by step, she looks down at her feet. Left foot, right foot, left foot, right foot: one after the other. A thought then pops into her mind:

She knows the gym so well (after all, she goes every day) that she could probably make her way safely down the stairs even if she were blindfolded.

She reaches the bottom of the steps and knows that she's arrived at the pool because the smell of chlorine is so penetrating that it assaults her senses. Before she can pay too much attention to the smell, she realizes with irritation that her towel is poking out of the gym bag once again. She simply sees to this by forcefully yanking around the contents of the bag until everything is sealed in tight.

She proceeds to put down her bag and then begins to put on her swimming cap. She manages to get all of her abundant hair uncomfortably (but neatly) tucked away. Finally she looks up and notices the pool.

More specifically, she sees a wolf sitting at the edge of the pool. Her eyes quickly dart back and forth as she realizes that she is in danger. The wolf isn't doing anything other than looking at her, and in an instant she realizes that it must have been watching her in absolute stillness and silence the *entire time*. This recognition of being seen leaves her feeling deeply unsettled.

It looks at her. And now she can do nothing other than look back at it. She wants to run but her legs simply won't move. In sheer disbelief she watches as the wolf stands up onto its hind legs, motioning to her to jump in and swim.

She wakes up sweating and in terror. But she is finally alive.

ABBY'S WOLF AND EMOTIONS
THAT MUST NOT BE EATEN

As you've just read, Abby woke up from her dream feeling very scared. Her fear was a visceral response to her psyche finally getting through to her via her dream. In the months building up to her dream she hadn't felt a thing. Her dream, uncomfortable as it was, flooded her with emotion because in her everyday life she had been denying how she felt.

Her dream didn't mean that danger was imminent in the near future. It was not precognitive in any sense. Her dream came to protect her from continuing to choose to move forward in the manner to which she was accustomed. To help her to reconnect to her instinctive nature and in doing so reinvite play, joy, creativity, love, laughter, and sex in her life. Her dream spoke to her to unleash the barriers within her life and psyche.

Healing the connection to your instinctive nature doesn't necessarily mean burning foundational structures down to the ground. It may simply mean that you have some altering to do. Sometimes this looks like intentionally putting up, and communicating, boundaries with certain people in your life. Other times it's simply a letting go of a stagnant inner belief.

For many people it means nurturing the sacredness of spirit openly. Extreme control always siphons off life and when it does, that may mean metaphorically burning those structures down!

There isn't an ideal "seven step program" on how to alter your life for the better when you have lost touch with your instincts. It is contradictory to the instinctive nature to even attempt to delineate it. You will have to navigate your own choices in relation to whichever cycle you find yourself in. But I will say this: time can act as your ally.

Take the time you need to reconnect to your own instincts and then make the changes in the best way you see fit. Remember that your instinctive, wild, deeply intuitive nature will edge you forward in ways that your rational mind may not understand.

If you realize that your emotions are out of whack. If you feel lost. If you feel angry. If you feel bitter. If you are seething. If you feel stuck. If you feel confused. If you feel nothing. If you feel your heart has burst into tiny shards of glass, filling up your chest with pain, then pay attention to your dreams because they will act as a healing balm.

They will guide you forward through the imagery you see and, most importantly, through the emotions they stir within you. Redirecting you to what you need most. That is, redirecting you back to your most instinctive and creative nature.

If the dream imagery is harsh, violent, and turbulent, all the more reason to pay attention to what is choked off, limited, and bubbling under the bedrock that is your life.

For Abby, that meant rediscovering who she was. She found it immensely helpful to think about what she loved to do before she became a mother and a wife. She released her self-imposed hold on having to be the "perfect mom." She rediscovered her sexuality—a process she thoroughly enjoyed.

She added a nonnegotiable practice of spending time every day to check in with how she was really feeling. She ate without criticizing herself and she found herself a pack of women who became real friends. She stopped competing and started connecting.

None of this happened overnight; in fact it took many months. But time became irrelevant because she was in her life, experiencing it, and not drudging through it like a carcass of a woman.

When you radically admit the truth to yourself is when things can actually change. You cannot tie a bow around bullshit and call it a bouquet. So no matter where you currently stand in relation to your instinctive nature, know this:

Your dream life will show you the way back. It will tell you when it is time to rest, push, fight, love, or let go. It will tell you exactly how to transform and transmute whatever it is that holds you back.

The instinctive nature is about *feeling your way* through. Perhaps you can spend an afternoon outside lounging in the sun. Or an evening dancing under the stars so that you heart is tended to. Maybe you could allow yourself to forget about what you look like and just enjoy your body. Remember: tending to the instinctive nature isn't a one-off thing but doing just one soulful creative action can reawaken your connection to it.

THE INSTINCTIVE NATURE IS NOT CONCERNED WITH GENDER

The instinctive nature is within us all—regardless of how we identify—and although I offered the previous story as a feminine example, anyone can lose their connection to their instinctive nature. Many people are socialized into stereotypical thinking, like solely focusing on making money or creating a home. This can result in a loss of the instinctive nature if there is no room for the person to explore all facets of themselves.

I've seen many men suffer the loss of their instinctive nature because they had been raised to become "real" men who did not show vulnerability. Society has let down men in many ways too. Men forget that they are also allowed to cultivate a rich inner life. That they are granted permission to be more than just "real" men and that they can step out of the focus of the rat race of domination, even if just momentarily, to feed their soulful inner needs.

If you are convincing yourself that you will begin to really start living or doing "X, Y, and Z" when you reach that goal, then perhaps you can simply acknowledge how you feel right now. If you tend to your inner life, you will begin to feel more alive, no matter what circumstances you find yourself in.

There will never be a perfect time when everything lines up. When, finally, you'll be able to enjoy your life. The more closely that you listen to your instinctive nature, the more enjoyable your journey will be on the way to your goal. Your instinctive nature is magnetic but it requires authentic living—that is, for us all.

DREAMS FACILITATE HEALING WHEN YOU NEED IT AND OFTEN REGARDLESS OF WHETHER YOU THINK IT IS CONVENIENT

When you feel disconnected from your instinctive nature, it is quite common to have dreams in which you are being chased or threatened in some way. Particularly when you are feeling emotionally overwhelmed in your everyday life. It's also common to have dreams of animals that are in danger or are injured in some way and need help. Usually the way that you tend to the injured animal is indicative of your current ability to facilitate inner healing.

Alternatively, you could dream that someone or something outside of you saves you (or attempts to save you). Both versions are indicative of transmutation, that is, an injured lamb is nurtured so that it can once again walk. An eagle flies over you and attacks a cloaked dream figure that is chasing you. Assistance comes in the form of whatever dream image is most poignant for you personally.

You will also come to discover that it's quite common to dream of wonderful "animal experiences" when you are in harmony with your instincts. For example, a dream wherein you are comfortably riding a beautiful horse in the direction you want to take.

Alternatively, if you have no clue where you are headed, and the horse is galloping forward at an alarming rate, the dream may be alerting you to the fact that you are being ruled by your desires and inner drives. That you need to regain control of your more basic desires in your waking life.

Let's break down Abby's dream for clarity as it is symbolically rich with meaning and message.

She is at a gym—a place she knows well. (The gym is representative of her psyche.) She isn't concerned about the people or distractions of the gym. She is concerned with her gym bag and all the stuff that keeps trying to pop out of the bag. (The bag is representative of her emotional state.)

She is shoving everything down. In other words she is trying to keep all her emotions contained. But that damn pesky towel, an item that keeps her warm and dry, keeps bursting out. Her emotions need to be released and they will find a way to be let out, just like the towel does.

She descends the stairs to the pool and has the thought that she could make her way blindfolded. (She can navigate the descent into the layers of her own psyche instinctively and intuitively—she doesn't need to actively see where she is going.) She locks up her beautiful hair into an uncomfortable swimming cap. (Hair is often representative of sexuality and/or strength in both dreams and stories.)

She reaches the pool. (The pool is symbolic of her unconscious because she had to climb down stairs to reach it. If the pool had been on the top floor it may have meant something different.)

She then sees a lone wolf that beckons to her to jump in and swim. A clear message to pay attention to her unconscious, her emotions, her intuition (the pool and swimming) and to find her instincts once again (to discover the wolf within)! The core message of the dream was for her to rekindle the connection to her instinctive nature.

Like Abby, your dreams are equally offering you guidance as to how to use your emotions and thoughts for healing and well-being.

THE ROLE OF DREAMS IN THE PROCESS OF TRANSFORMATION & REBIRTH

In Abby's waking life she experienced a catharsis. She let go of all that pent-up emotion. As a direct result of her dream guidance, she made the necessary life changes so that she could stop faking it and actually feel good! And don't we want to feel good as much as we can?

When your emotions are blocked, your instincts are naturally suppressed and with that the connection to your intuition is also stifled. If you close up or dam up the connection to your emotions, you will feel stuck. This is also the case for the opposite end of the spectrum. If you express all your emotions in whatever shape or form without thought of consequence, then you will also feel disconnected.

In the latter case, you're stuck in emotional purging. Just think of someone who can't seem to contain their frustration or anger and always regrets it after. Or people whose emotions are so hostile that they dominate their interactions and relationships regardless of the other person's emotions and feelings.

In scenarios like this, the dream will show the dreamer symbols that speak to this unregulated emotion. A person experiencing uncapped rage may dream of a mass murderer who relentlessly pursues them.

Or the dream symbol will provide the dreamer with emotional regulation in the form of a symbolic opposite. An emotionally explosive person may dream of very serene landscapes and bodies of water with which they interact. (If there is a monster lurking in the water that the dreamer suddenly becomes aware of, that shows the dreamer that they are dealing with something below the surface of their conscious awareness. The monster within is now ready to be seen and witnessed. That is, their dream alerts them to the possibility of facing the "emotional monster" instead of running away from it.)

That said, dream symbols that highlight emotional well-being often appear as containers. In Abby's dream her gym bag is the symbolic container! It can be any type of container, such as cars, bags, or even Tupperware. There's a good reason for this: containers are symbolic vessels that hold content within them. In this case, emotional content.

When we do not feel emotionally contained, we generally do not feel safe in the presence of the full spectrum of our emotions and life experiences. So our dreams come to alert us to the state of our own ability to witness, experience, and embrace (contain) our emotions and life experiences. We therefore dream of containment symbols like baskets, bags, and even coffins—usually in different states or conditions.

In other words, dream images and symbols signify how emotionally safe the dreamer feels. For example, if the symbolic dream containers are broken, old, and falling apart, then the dreamer's emotional patterns are likely the same. They may feel threatened, broken, burned-out, buried, and emotionally unsupported.

We all need to be emotionally seen and heard. Our dreams speak to how much we feel we are, or are not, receiving that kind of emotional acknowledgment, love, and support, both from ourselves and the people we are in relationships with.

So if you are emotionally closed off, or at the mercy of everything you feel, there is an imbalance. This isn't to say that you shouldn't feel how you feel. In fact it's the opposite. Feel your feelings but know that they are temporary in their fluidity of expression.

If you get stuck in a chronic way of emotional relating or expression, then you've fallen out of alignment. This happens to all of us from time to time—so this isn't something to feel bad about. Our dream work simply helps us to get back into alignment more quickly.

Getting into emotional alignment and balance often requires a release. A letting go of handling things in the same old way. A freeing of what has been stored up in excess; a catharsis of sorts. If we allow it, we can arrive at a point where transformation can occur. That is, once the emotion (the one hiding behind the trigger, the experience, that person, or the past) is fully acknowledged, felt, confronted, and then released. We see this clearly in the case of Tidal Wave dreams.

THE TIDAL WAVE DREAM

At its core the Tidal Wave Dream is a dream centered around one image (called the central image) that leaves the dreamer feeling helpless. Despite the name, the central image doesn't always have to be a tidal wave (although in many cases it actually is!). It can be a fire, a group of terrifying militant men, or a tornado, for example. It is simply one core image that dominates your dream and is distressing to experience.

The term was coined by eminent researcher Dr. Ernest Hartmann. From his research and work with countless patients he realized that people who had experienced a trauma in their waking lives would often go on to experience a type of dream that he called the Tidal Wave Dream.

In its truest form the tidal wave in the dream isn't specifically about replaying a traumatic event or memory over again. It's about the mind's ability to create a new image. That is, to help the dreamer emotionally adapt to what has happened by highlighting the dominant emotion and feelings that are permeating their life.

A tidal wave would render anyone helpless, so the idea is not about conquering the fear but rather processing it and experiencing, or re-experiencing, feelings of vulnerability in a way that is actually helpful, by having the dreamer acknowledge *and progress through* how they feel.

So if you've experienced a Tidal Wave Dream it's a clear sign to really pour on the self-compassion and look at what needs to be healed. It may also be helpful to get external, professional assistance to help you manage the process of your healing.

If you are sitting in fear as a direct consequence of having experienced a trauma, please know that your dreams aren't trying to hurt you! Your mind is not against you. Rather, your whole being is trying to make sense of a terrible event and in the process attempting to recalibrate you to a place of well-being. Your dreams are actively part of that recalibrating and healing process.

Once again, often in our dreams frightening and flooding emotions are brought to our attention, in whatever way necessary, so that we can transform them for the better. It's not surprising to me that these types of dreams often come in the form of engulfing water because when you are rendered helpless, you are literally flooded with emotion that is inescapable. The healing work then lies in releasing this flood of emotion before it gets stored in the body.

It is important to bring your dream material to light by addressing what you've been through and knowing how you actually feel. You don't need to begin this process alone—reach out and get support. Know that there are many pathways to healing and even more to once again experience joy and well-being.

EVERYDAY EMOTIONAL REGULATION VIA DREAMS

Regular experiences, that is, non-traumatic experiences and the emotions connected to them, also influence our dreams. In fact many scientific studies have proven this to be true, specifically in the work done by Dr. Rosalinda D. Cartwright. Just think about how many times you've experienced something emotionally charged (either positive or negative) during the course of your day, only to then have a dream about it later that night or that week.

For example, maybe you met someone great at the gym and then later that night you dream that you are at a concert with them. Or maybe your neighbor made an off-hand remark to you, which you laughed off at the time, only to then find yourself driving them to the hospital in your dreams.

Your dreams help to regulate your emotions without your conscious effort. Dr. Cartwright's scientific research highlights the significance and benefits of this: over the course of one night most of us have many different types of dreams, and these lessen in emotional intensity as the night progresses. It's often why we wake up feeling better than when we went to bed. Our dreams help us to process our emotions over the course of the night, lessening their intensity, and altering them into memory. (Luckily, this also happens every night regardless of whether we can actually remember our dreams the next day!)

Ultimately, our dreams are guiding us all toward greater well-being. So whether you are in alignment with well-being or not, you will find that your dreams will help to regulate how you feel. You can simply focus on getting a good night's rest and let your dreams do the work for you!

FEELING GOOD AND THE HONESTY OF EMOTIONS

I can imagine that some of you, like me, sometimes think that it is just impossible to feel good. The death of a loved one, a bad day, an illness, a stillbirth, a loss of income, a pandemic—these are all hard experiences to go through. And the difficulty of them should not be covered up with positive platitudes.

Being in touch with your emotions isn't about pretending to feel good when things are bad. Sometimes feeling good is just about being able to expand the space between external stimuli and response.

Many times, greater well-being is simply recognizing that you have the power to choose well-being even in devastating situations. To choose self-compassion instead of debilitating guilt and self-criticism because you once again find yourself in a situation you would rather not be in.

There is no emotion that is unhelpful. Emotional strength is about being able to move through the expression of emotion without getting stuck. Anger is a powerful motivator and protector when boundaries are violated. Grief, an honoring of love well experienced. Sadness, a key to pivoting. Rage, a call to tear down limiting structures. All these emotions guide us to greater well-being. Emotions are not final destinations. They are fluid markers of the experience of life.

When we do the emotional work, we then naturally feel good, without having to mentally convince ourselves that we do. In the moment of experiencing fun, love, and joy, you don't affirm over and over: I am joyful, I am joyful. You simply feel it to the fullest capacity of your being.

Yet, when we are in the dark, that is when it is helpful to remind ourselves: I know joy. I know joy. I know joy. It's choosing over and over again, by allowing your feelings to move through you, to align yourself with well-being even when it feels impossible to do so.

WARNING DREAMS AND WELL-BEING

In their book, *Dreams That Can Save Your Life: Early Warning Signs of Cancer and Other Diseases*, authors Larry Burk, M.D. and Kathleen O'Keefe-Kanavos share stories and evidence of people who had dreams signaling that something was wrong with their health, which later turned out to be true. One particular story comes from a woman named Diane.

Diane had an incredibly vivid dream about having surgery to remove a cancerous lump in her breast. So much so that on waking she booked an appointment for a mammogram. A couple of days later she went for that appointment where she discovered that she did indeed have cancer. She was astounded—as was her doctor. The book is filled with examples of first-person accounts of people who had dreams that warned them about some form of illness that later proved to be accurate through medical testing.

Here's a key factor to these warning dreams. All the people in the book *knew* that there was something significant to that dream. It didn't feel like their other dreams. Their dreams were not the result of "day residue" or anxiety. Meaning they didn't watch a film, or speak to a friend who had cancer (for example) that then made them feel anxious, so that later that night they dreamed about experiencing it themselves. Their dreams were experientially different than usual; they felt important, shook the dreamers to their core, and generally came out of the blue.

We cannot definitively prove whether their dreams were a loud message from the Universe or simply a repressed inner knowing coming to light in the dream world. What we do know, though, is that their dreams literally saved their lives because they were propelled to take action on the guidance they received. Advice for us all.

In your regular dreams you too could be warned of something that you need to pay attention to and should address. It doesn't necessarily have to be about your health; it can be about the safety of your loved ones, for example.

This was the case for physicist and aerospace engineer Dale E. Graff, who had a particularly startling dream. In his dream he saw a car blow up. In the dream he was cognizant of the fact that he recognized that the car was the same make as his wife's car. He knew that the car in his dream wasn't a symbolic reflection of his emotional state. In other words, he wasn't dreaming about the car blowing up because he was angry with his wife. He had not denied any anger in his waking life.

So as a precautionary measure he took her car to a mechanic for an inspection. A few days later, the mechanic called Graff and said, "You were driving a time bomb!" The mechanic had discovered that there was an error with the fuel pump and the gas tank, and in fact the car could have blown up if they had left the issue unattended. Graff dreamed of a probable future, and subsequently through action experienced a different one.

Our regular dreams are rich in healing, insight, and warning if necessary.

PRACTICAL EXERCISE #1: CULTIVATING EMOTIONAL LIBERATION AND CREATIVE SOLUTIONS THROUGH THE PRACTICE OF DREAM INCUBATION

If you feel stuck as to how to get over an emotional hurdle, you can use dream incubation in order to garner clarity. In fact, you can use dream incubation for any problem that you are experiencing. That is because we are in a state of egoic nonresistance when we dream, which makes it easier to gain insight.

I've witnessed countless people gain insight into repetitive patterns of behavior, self-sabotage, fears, triggering family connections, and so forth with incredible clarity in their incubated dreams. So much so that it becomes much easier to address the issues on waking and in doing so, to move toward joy and greater personal well-being.

Simply put, dream incubation is a method in which you visualize the dream experience you want to have *before you go to bed*. In essence, you prime your dream(s) before you fall asleep. Dream incubation is an ancient and effective visualization technique because it helps you to focus your attention. And in doing so can help you to receive creative solutions to any of the problems that you may be experiencing.

In order to incubate your regular dreams you simply need to set the intention for guidance and clarity before you fall asleep. As a practice, you could mentally repeat the following statement before you fall asleep: "I will dream of what my life purpose is. Once I have received this guidance I will wake up immediately."

Get your energy in balance before you go to bed, then, when you are ready, focus on nothing else but your intention. Hone your intention as you begin to feel like you are about to fall asleep. As distracting thoughts arise simply witness them and go back to repeating your intention. Mentally say your intention over and over again until you fall asleep. You may find that you need do this entire exercise for a couple of nights in a row. Persevere with this practice if you don't get results immediately.

Many of my clients have had high success doing this simple exercise. The trick here is to be incredibly mindful of the words you choose. It has also been my experience that in the dream state our words have even more power than in waking life, so it is even more important to use them wisely.

For example, I once had a client who used the following intention: "My dreams will help me to discover my music." He repeated his intention, over and over, like a mantra, before he fell asleep. He then went on to dream about his intention, but in the form of him searching and searching for his music.

He woke up feeling highly exhausted because he had spent the entire dream evening running from one production studio to another. Night after night he experienced a similar state of searching but never discovered his music. That is, not until he changed the way he worded his intention.

His intention simply wasn't clear enough. He pivoted and used the following intention with success: "I hear and experience my original music tonight." That night he dreamed of being in a coffee shop where he purchased his track on iTunes and then listened to it. On waking he could remember the music he heard and went on to write the sheet music for it.

If I'm struggling with an emotional situation I will say: "As the energy that creates my dreams, please show me the purpose of this grief." And then I'll dream of a corresponding picture that shows me what I am missing in my waking life or generally what I need to let go of. Sometimes the imagery will be abstract or, at other times, I hear a disembodied voice speak to me clarifying what I need to know.

It's been my experience that difficult emotions often come up as pictures (or even colors) that convey messages alerting me to what is required. I have never experienced the same dream setting twice unless I have actively gone on to influence the dreamscape through becoming lucid in my dreams.

This process may be completely different for you. Trust the process of your dream incubation. Equally, if you incubate your dream for guidance and get a nonsensical answer, or don't get any answer, then focus on healing in your waking life and then try again when you feel ready.

PRACTICAL EXERCISE #2: USE YOUR WAKING IMAGINATION TO FURTHER EXPLORE YOUR EMOTIONAL NARRATIVES

If you feel that your dream was particularly poignant and would like to explore it further, simply do this exercise at a time when you will not be disturbed. You may also find it helpful to go through your dream journal to pick a dream that stands out for you.

Step 1: Recall your dream to the best of your ability. Imagine the dream scenario playing out in your mind without actively influencing it.

Step 2: When you feel ready, begin to alter your dream as you see fit. You can change anything. After a couple of minutes what generally happens is that your imagination will take over.

Step 3: Stay in this process for as long as you like.

Step 4: When you feel like the process is over, simply write down what you experienced.

Step 5: Once you've written down your dream, highlight any particular changes that stood out for you.

Step 6: Pay attention to how you feel about these modifications: Did your waking dream take a dramatic turn (or change!) that surprised you?

Step 7: Then ask: What action can I take?

One of the goals of this exercise is to join, and balance, any conflicting forces within your mind and at the same time process any of the emotions that naturally arise. Another advantage of this exercise is that it can point you in the direction of your limits and strengths so that you can cultivate greater inner cohesiveness.

The imagery that comes up is insightful and helpful. For example, did you take your dream and play out a terrible ending? Did an average dream become exceptional? Did a certain person show up again despite your best intentions to keep them out of your mind? This exercise will show you which of your dreams need to be shattered and which dreams need to be nurtured. If you prefer, you can also resolve any scary or limiting dreams by practicing the exercise on facing shadow figures in chapter eight, which walks you through exactly how to do that.

CHAPTER 3

THE SYMBOLIC LANGUAGE OF DREAM INTERPRETATION

It's a Wednesday morning and I've just woken up from a really vivid dream. In my dream I'm alone in my car driving on a wide-open road. I'm happily singing along to music that's playing on the radio when I look into the rearview mirror, only to see a black jaguar staring back at me. In complete disbelief I bring my car to a sudden and complete halt.

I turn around to see, *really see*, if there is actually a jaguar sitting in the backseat of my car while my mind races with a flurry of questions. How can a jaguar be in my car? How did it get in here? What if it tries to eat me? Is it going to hurt me? Is it going to attack me? Should I just jump out of the car?

The jaguar, on the other hand, doesn't look perturbed in the slightest about me or my shock. It simply places its paw on the seat belt (which it is neatly strapped into) patiently waiting for me to calm down. It looks me straight in the eye and as it does I feel that it's peering into the depths of my being.

As this is all happening, a type of fear mixed with anticipation begins to rise up within me. The jaguar opens its mouth to tell me something and I know it's important. I'm ready to hear what it has to say.

And in that very moment I wake up.

Some dreams just feel different. They carry an emotional weight to them—a gravity that demands attention. My jaguar dream commanded my attention, and to this day, many years later, it still remains one of the most powerful dream experiences I've had. Specifically because of its symbolic message but also because of what happened next.

At the time of my jaguar dream I was twenty-two, unemployed, and firmly entrenched in the process of trying to figure it all out. I worked so many odd jobs, none of which I really enjoyed, only to end up feeling even more confused and deflated. At the time of my dream my indecision was really coming to a head because of external pressures to get my life sorted out.

In order to distract myself from my dream and from my life situation, I decided to visit a center filled with lovely coffee shops and boutique-style clothing stores. While I was meandering around I noticed a beautiful secondhand bookshop and decided to go in. I absolutely love the essence of secondhand bookstores: a mixture of time forgotten and new possibilities all patiently awaiting you, if only you look!

I began to slowly move through the store, indulging in all the books that I picked up as I went along. As I turned a corner the manager, a blond woman in her late forties, started to walk toward me with a pile of books in her hands. She then handed me a few books and told me to take a look at them because they were on sale.

Slightly taken aback, and before I could even respond, she was off speaking to another customer. The book on the top of the pile was *Jaguar Woman: The Wisdom of the Butterfly Tree*, written by Lynn V. Andrews. In total awe of the synchronicity that had just happened, I of course promptly purchased the book. In that moment it became clear to me that I needed to pay attention to all of the symbolic messages that were being sent my way, both in my waking life and in my dreams.

My experience showed me that symbolic guidance from the Universe can follow through from dreams into waking life. It also showed me that there is no barrier in our ability to receive guidance other than our unwillingness to pay attention to it. That means that the Universe will also send you as many messages as it takes until you click. That is, both in your life and in your dreams!

Most of us make our dreams and the Universe work very hard to get our attention. We need big, bold messages so obvious in nature (but totally unanticipated) to even begin to believe that we are being communicated with. I was the perfect example of this: I had received guidance in the form of my dream but simply chose to ignore it!

I didn't honor my dream by spending the time needed to listen to and interpret it. Instead I just shrugged it off, choosing distraction over clarity once again. Yet, the jaguar symbol stalked my waking life too, making it impossible to ignore its message. Had I listened to my dream I would have recognized that I had already been shown the path forward. I would have seen that my dream had already offered me all the answers that I needed.

In the dream I was driving on a wide-open road (a symbol of wide possibilities). There weren't any other cars or obstructions in the road (symbolically: my path was clear). I was driving the car and happily singing to music at the same time (symbolically: I'm at the wheel of my life and the journey can be joyful).

Then I saw the jaguar strapped neatly into the backseat of my car. In many ancient cultures the jaguar is a symbol of power often associated with healing and shamanic initiation. The fact that it was in the backseat of my car showed me that my inner power had metaphorically taken a backseat in my life.

The jaguar didn't hurt me. In fact it was about to tell me something very important, which I started to get excited about, only to then wake up! At the time of this dream I wasn't a very experienced lucid dreamer. Had I been, I would have incubated another dream in order to hear what the jaguar had to say to me.

My regular dream was showing me what I needed to know anyway! I had tucked my power away by not taking any action to help myself. My fear, it turned out, wasn't that I couldn't make good choices, or that I was either "lost" or "stuck." It was that I had access to a type of inner strength and power that could change everything. A gift that both frightened and excited me.

My reaction to the jaguar in my dream blatantly highlighted my internal conflict. In the dream I mentally questioned whether the jaguar was going to attack me, hurt me, or even eat me. I even toyed with the thought of jumping out of the car—talk about avoidance!

In other words, the way in which I approached the jaguar in the dream was how I was actually approaching an aspect of myself in my life. The dream highlighted the choice I was facing: Was I going to continue avoiding my power or was I going to claim it and use it?

I recognized that my indecision and commonplace excuse of being "lost" was simply my fear in disguise. I was so afraid of making the wrong career choice that I unintentionally forced myself to become stuck. I had completely dismissed my spiritual strength and sight— and was actively holding myself in a lockdown of no movement!

Life changes when we choose to change. That is when we use our inner strength to face where we are in reality and decide to move forward despite any fears and limiting beliefs.

I reclaimed my own emotional power and life vitality by choosing to re-enroll into a university program. At the same time, I studied with a shamanic guide who helped me explore different spiritual teachings and practices to expand my own energy. I got a part-time job at a retail store so that I could financially assist myself. And most importantly, I ended a relationship that was clearly not working, and fully embraced being single.

The entire process of moving forward then became more enjoyable because I wasn't fixating on what could happen in the future. I wasn't trying to create certainty out of the unknown. I was simply taking one healthy step forward a day at a time while actively learning how to embrace the mystery of the unknown. The epitome of what the black jaguar does in the jungle, too. Its symbolic message is apparent: embrace the dark mystery and hunt as if it's clear.

DREAMS ARE A FORM OF SYMBOLIC STORYTELLING

As you've seen, everything in a dream appears symbolically. From the dream characters, and how they interact with you, to the actual dream scenery that shows up nightly. There are no mistakes as far as the symbols that appear in our dreams.

They are specific, purposeful, and timely.

Even if we cannot immediately understand or intuit the imagery or message held within the dream, the symbols that you dream of are still significant. Dream messages are designed to help us heal, create, and positively move forward.

Like all dream symbolism, the manner in which you approach it matters. You only need to do a quick internet search for "dream symbolism" to see that there are more than one billion search results. There is such a large collective drive to understand the symbols that we experience in both our waking and dream lives because we instinctively know that symbols hold great insight and meaning!

Over a billion search results also tell us that there are many, many different opinions as to how to go about deciphering dream symbols and the messages they contain. I use two very specific methods to decode dream messages, both of which merge psychological insight with spiritual intuition. The first is my ABC (Accept, Believe, Clarify) method of dream interpretation. The second is a more traditional thematic model of dream interpretation. Shortly, I'm going to show you exactly how to use both of these dream interpretation techniques.

In order to accurately interpret your own dream messages you need to work with both the psychological and spiritual elements of your dreams and your life. Emotions, thoughts, everyday experiences, and personal history can be seen to fall under a psychological framework that you use when you are decoding your dream messages.

Then the collective history, your energetic vibration, intuitive insight, and future manifestations all fall under a spiritual framework of understanding that you also use to decode your dream messages. There is a no real division between these two frameworks other than the one I've just created for ease of understanding.

All dreams act as the *unio mystica*. This means that dreams are the medium through which opposites are integrated: the psychological and spiritual. The masculine and feminine. The physical and non-physical. The unconscious and the conscious. Thoughts and emotions. All factors together, none more valid than the other.

Let's take a look at my jaguar dream to see this in action. My dream was just a regular dream. Or so I thought! Yet, the dream symbols were greatly influenced by the Universe. This was later proven evident in my experience of synchronicity. My dream was a spiritual message showing me how to overcome my emotional and psychological barriers. That is, barriers of limiting belief and fear. It was spirit and psyche working together.

Your psyche and your spirit are not split; as always, it is simply perception that clouds this union. Right now, I would love for you to just take a moment to think about your own dreams in relation to what you are currently experiencing in your life. Can you see that your dreams are always talking to what is happening for you as a spiritual being in a physical body? Ultimately, your dreams are always moving you toward greater wholeness and well-being.

We see evidence of this when we have prophetic or precognitive dreams that speak either about our own lives or about the collective we live in. For example, prior to the terror attacks that happened on 9/11, many people had strange and unnerving dreams involving the imagery of towers. One woman dreamed of a tower made of skeletons with ash surrounding it. Another dreamed of two pterodactyls (phonetically sounds like TERROR-dak-till) flying and circling around two identical tall buildings or towers. These are just two examples of collective numinous dreams. There are many more.

Dreams show us our link to spirit and the greater vantage point we can access by simply being connected. They also speak to us about the connection that we intrinsically have to one another and the whole of life around us. Not just in times of crisis and trauma but also during times of well-being. In fact, at all times. Through nurturing all of our dream messages we are able to thrive both internally and externally, as well as individually and collectively.

THE ABC METHOD TO DECODING YOUR DREAM MESSAGES

The goal of my "ABC" (Accept, Believe, Clarify) method is to help you to gain immediate insight into your dream experiences. Unlike the thematic method of dream interpretation, which revolves around decoding longstanding patterns of behavior, the ABC method is designed to help you view your dream as an instant well of guidance and immediate resource of assistance.

With the ABC method of dream interpretation you need to look at your dream as a complete story *in relation to where you currently find yourself.* My golden rule for this form of dream interpretation is to always ask the following question: *Why this dream, in this way, right now?*

Now I'm going to offer you a dream story from a workshop participant of mine who has graciously allowed me to share it with you. Try and interpret it before you move on to the ABC method of explanation of the dream. My recommendation is simply offered to let you get a feel for your own level of dream interpretation skill. The dream is as follows:

> *I'm driving my car when I clearly come to a red light. Instead of stopping at the traffic light I put my foot on the pedal and jump the crossroad. I see the other cars hurtling toward me and I think they're going to hit me. Yet somehow I make it to the other side of the road! My heart is pumping in my chest as I decide to go home. I wake up shortly after that.*

What do you think the dream message is here? A story of hope or simply an anxiety-based dream? Let's explore the dream message using the ABC method.

STEP 1: ACCEPT AND ACKNOWLEDGE ALL OF THE SYMBOLS WITHIN THE DREAM

In this dream, the dreamer is clearly dealing with six dream symbols. They are:

1. The red traffic light

2. The car

3. The crossroad

4. The other cars

5. Fear and anticipation

6. Their home

If we condense the dream message, this is what we know: The dreamer is at a crossroad. They make a risky decision to jump the red traffic light despite the approach of other cars. The dreamer gets to the other side safely and is relieved about this. The dreamer then decides to go home.

STEP 2: BELIEVE THAT THE DREAM HAS YOUR BEST INTEREST AT HEART

The dream is a message of risk-taking and the potential consequences thereof. How do we know that? Because jumping a red traffic light is simply a big risk. As an outside person interpreting the dream, we remain in the dark as to what the actual risk-taking is in relation to. What is clear, though, is that the dreamer is at a crossroad and that the risk is somehow linked to the choice that they make.

Crossroads, as dream symbols, are significant because they reveal the importance of making decisions with our eyes wide open. They symbolically signify four choices, simply because of their structure. You can go left, right, forward, or backward. A crossroad is also a cardinal, or fundamental, symbol that often holds religious connotations regardless of whether the dreamer is religious. That is because of the "cross" implicit in the term.

The dreamer is at a red light and decides to go forward regardless of the risk. Red lights in life are actual symbols of stopping. In the dream the dreamer "breaks the law" (perhaps a cardinal law because the traffic light is on the cross?) and jumps the red light. Luckily, they make it safely to the other side without getting hit by any of the other cars. The dreamer's heart pumps as they make the decision to go home.

All dreams offer us positive guidance even if the symbols appear on the surface to be negative. As I mentioned earlier you should always use your dream interpretation for positive benefit. This is a critical step in the ABC method—to believe that your dream is giving you a message of benevolence. So, if this dream has the dreamer's best interest at heart, what is the core message?

The dreamer is at a crossroad in their life. They are faced with a decision that is (or feels) risky and that likely involves breaking the rules. The dream is alerting the dreamer to the consequence of their risk-taking (first in thought) before they do so in reality. No matter the risk, at the end of it all they choose to return home—as evident at the end of the dream.

Would it interest you to know that this dream is actually from a client of mine, who was on the precipice of starting an extramarital affair with someone they work with? Things become so much clearer when you interpret dreams in relation to what is actually happening in your life! *That is why you should always ask yourself: Why this dream, in this way, right now?*

Now, let's return to my client's dream but this time equipped with the additional information of the potential affair:

The dreamer is at a crossroad in their life. Will they choose to cheat? In their dream the red traffic light represents societal rules of behavior (abiding by monogamy). We know that the traffic light is a societal symbol because we all have to stop at red lights. . . . They don't abide by the rules; they jump the light (they emotionally/physically want to take the risk and have the affair). Their dream is acknowledging their sexual desire and wants.

The other cars drive at them in the dream. The cars could represent people who could find out about the affair or perhaps even represent her own internalized judgment of their desire. They could also be seen as phallic sexual symbols.

Regardless of the danger of the cars they make it safely to the other side of the crossroad. In other words, they come out of the situation unscathed. They feel their heart pumping in their chest (adrenaline inducing action, much like having an affair). They then decide to go home (they choose to return to their partner).

STEP 3: CLARIFY YOUR ACTION STEP

The dream isn't a message of judgment; it's a message of clarity of action. The dreamer would likely get away with cheating because their dream tells them so. They make it to the other side unscathed! BUT they are torn by the decision to cheat and so their dream assists them by playing out their internal conflict. This doesn't mean that they have to remain faithful to their partner (or that they should or shouldn't). Their dream simply speaks to the effect their risk-taking—the affair—would likely have on their life. That said, their action step in the dream was clear: they willingly return home.

UNPACKING THE ABC METHOD OF DREAM DECODING

If you use my ABC method of dream interpretation, it is important that you view your dreams in relation to what is actually happening in your life. Your dreams are a well of guidance that will guide you through all of your experiences. In order to do good dream work you simply need to acknowledge that all dreams are actually offering you great insight for both immediate issues and long-standing matters.

Even though my client dreamed of universal and collective dream symbols (the cars and the road) they were significant to her particular situation.

Now imagine that the dreamer was actually a forty-three-year-old man who was undergoing chemotherapy for an aggressive cancer at the time of his dream. Then the dream would take on an entirely different meaning even though the dream imagery would remain the same. An example:

He is at a red light (his cancer diagnosis). He finds himself at a crossroad (that is, the precipice between illness and wellness or even life and death). He jumps the crossroad despite the other cars (the other cars could be representative of the aggressive cancer cells) hurtling toward him. He makes it to the other side (wellness). He is relieved and decides to go home.

The house as a symbol here represents the dreamer's body and spiritual home. The dream also shows the dreamer how they feel about their diagnosis and treatment. At the same time it acts as a form of spiritual reassurance, showing him that he makes it to the other side (he crosses over) and goes home.

When you decode your own dream messages using the ABC method, you need to first accept and acknowledge that all of the symbols in the dream are there to assist you. That means even the frightening symbols! Trust that the dream has your best interest at heart and use your interpretation in such a way that it benefits you.

Look at your dream as a story that is symbolically giving you a message through the imagery that you see, the actions you take, and the emotions you experience. Lastly, clarify your choice of action based on the guidance of your dream message so that you can move forward positively in your waking life.

THE THEMATIC METHOD OF DREAM INTERPRETATION AND ANALYSIS

This alternative method of dream interpretation is hinged on working with repetitive dream imagery and aimed at longer-term personal growth work. As such, it requires that you have a somewhat sizable collection of dream entries, unlike the ABC method, which can be used on just one dream. I recommend that you have at least a minimum of thirty dream entries before you begin to decode your dream messages in this way.

With any luck you followed the guidance offered to you at the beginning of this book imploring you to keep a dream journal. If you have, congratulations, you should now have a good collection of your dreams that you can begin to interpret! If you don't have a lot of dream entries, don't worry, simply bookmark this chapter and then come back to it once you are more ready.

This method of dream interpretation is specifically designed to help you identify any long-standing patterns of belief or behaviors that are no longer serving you. As a method, it really gets to the heart of your personal growth, because it shows you exactly what you need to look at, let go of, accept, or simply change for the better.

What you will also discover through doing this process of dream interpretation is that many of these beliefs, which may be outside of your current awareness, will begin to become apparent. As such, this process of dream interpretation is extremely illuminating. That is because you can only really move past an unhelpful pattern of behavior or belief once you actually know what it is!

WHEN TO DO THIS EXERCISE:

Do this exercise when you have a minimum of an hour to spare. This is very active personal growth work, so map out a time during which you won't be interrupted or disturbed. After all, you are going on a quest to discover the state of your inner world. I have also found that if I do this exercise with music on in the background, it influences the forms of themes I pick up on because of the lyrics. So just a heads-up: try and do this exercise with as few distractions as possible!

WHAT YOU'LL NEED:

You will need your dream journal, a few differently colored pens or highlighters, and a couple of sheets of paper. You can also download a free example of my dream journal sheets on my website (athenalaz.com).

DISCOVERING UNDERLYING THEMES THAT APPEAR IN YOUR DREAM ENTRIES

The core goal for you here is to notice any repetitive dream symbols, emotions, imagery, and places so that you can discover the themes that they collectively represent. You do this so that you can identify any long-standing patterns of behavior or beliefs that are trying to make themselves known to you through your dreams. You find these themes so that you can use them to grow and develop as a person.

The art of this form of dream interpretation is to simply let any repetitive symbols and imagery pop out at you. Don't hold on to any preconceived ideas of what you think you may discover. Simply begin the exercise with an open mind and zero expectations.

Using your colored highlighters or pens, mark any dream symbols that appear repetitively over the different dream entries that you've selected to work with. For example, you may notice that a "house" or a "hotel" appears in most of your dreams. You would then mark the house down as a repetitive symbol. Again the goal here is to scan your selected dream entries while highlighting any symbols that appear frequently over the course of different dreams.

Perhaps the dream elements of "water" or "fire" feature prominently in your dream entries. Maybe you notice that you are always wearing a specific item of clothing (jeans) or doing one particular action (driving, say) more often than not. Or alternatively, maybe you pick up that you use the words "afraid" and "anxious" repeatedly.

Whatever the case, simply follow this method to the point where you feel like you've exhausted all of the repetitive dream imagery that appears throughout the course of your different dream entries.

Then, reading over what you've highlighted, simply begin to make a list of all the repetitive symbols that you've noted. Write this list on one of the sheets of paper. Here is a list of symbols from a client of mine whose dream entries spanned the course of three months:

1. House

2. Pool

3. Afraid

4. Elevators

5. Car

6. Hotel

7. Train

8. Keys

9. Sea

10. Home

11. School

12. Ocean

13. Running away

14. Female drivers

15. People who I don't know in my waking life

16. My partner

17. Anxious

18. Parties

19. Events

The length of the list is irrelevant. What is important is that once you've listed all of the repetitive dream symbols, you then read over them again. This is so that you can see if they can be condensed down into more "nuclear" symbols. For example, the previous list can be further reduced as follows:

1. Pool/Ocean/Sea

2. House/Home/Hotel

3. Afraid/Anxious/Running (i.e., running away from something = avoidance)

4. Elevators/Keys

5. School

6. Car/Train/Female drivers

7. Strangers

8. My partner

9. Parties/Events

The core list of symbols should be made into singular themes. For example, you may recognize that "the sea," "the ocean," and "the pool" all embody and represent water. This means that the first identified theme is water.

Then you may discover that "houses," "homes," and "hotels" can be grouped together and are another theme. That is the state of your psyche. The next symbols that can be grouped together are the dreamer's repetitive emotions (anxious, afraid, or avoidant). These emotions can then be themed down to the way the dreamer deals with difficulties in their life (i.e., their coping strategies). And so it goes.

Try and connect an underlying theme to as many of the symbols as you can. Sometimes symbols can be grouped together and at other times they stand singularly. In this example, "school," "strangers," and the dreamer's "partner" cannot be grouped with the other symbols because they are not similar to the other symbols. As such they are singular symbols, each of which embodies its own theme.

For example, "school" could be themed down to represent past childhood experiences and/or any learning that the dreamer is currently undergoing. "Strangers" could be themed down to represent something new or unexpected that the dreamer is experiencing both internally and externally. The dreamer's partner is thematically representative of intimacy or, more simply, their partner.

The goal here is to approach these symbols in a very pragmatic and helpful way. Simply ask yourself: What do I associate this symbol with? Then ask: What does this symbol represent universally? Use both your intuition and your common sense.

The themes that you find are really bringing your attention to what needs to be integrated, changed, or transformed in your own life. If you are tempted to dismiss specific symbols and themes or if you have a very intense reaction to them—then definitely note them down.

These unwanted symbols are brilliant clues to your transformation and liberating change! They may not be the symbols that you would ideally choose but they're most definitely the ones you *need*! Symbolic themes that irk you also hold the keys to your personal freedom. If you have dreams where you are constantly in a messy house, then the dream is showing you that you need to clean up any clogged-up energy, beliefs, emotions, and/or behaviors. Ask: What's weighing me down? What mess do I need to clean up?

The ultimate goal of this exercise is to use these themes (aka your dream messages!) for greater personal growth. What is the point of getting inspiration and insight if you don't do anything with it? Use the information that you receive! Self-reflective questions can assist you in unpacking the themes that you discover. For example, if you recognize that one of the consistent themes throughout your dreams is avoidance, you could then ask:

What am I avoiding? Why am I avoiding this? Am I afraid of intimacy? Am I afraid of judgment or rejection? How would I feel if I did get what I wanted? What would happen if I said yes instead of no? How would my life change if I did find true love? Dig deep within yourself to discover what is holding you back. Allow your dreams to illuminate the path forward by shedding light on any hidden fears.

Perhaps you think that a new situation will end up like painful experiences that you lived through in the past. Or that you'll embarrassingly fail if you try something. Whatever the case, you can move past any inner obstacle by changing the way you relate to it and through the action that you take. If your dreams are alerting you to your avoidance, then in your waking life you could try and deliberately engage with the very experiences, emotions, or relationships that you have been avoiding.

If you are brave enough to try a new approach in your waking life, you will discover that your nighttime dreams will shift right along with you. *As always: dreams adapt to the dreamer!* That means that if you change your behavior in your waking life, your dream content will change too. For example, you may experience frightening dreams where you are being chased and having to run away, only to then have dreams of comfortable social interactions or even petting random animals.

If you find that you still struggle (like we all do) with difficult symbols, emotions, or themes, you can then invite them into your lucid
dreams, something we will explore together in chapter nine. Lucid
dreaming provides invaluable support in helping you to understand
why the symbol is difficult in the first place. You can simply ask your
lucid dream to show you a memory associated with what you are
struggling with. I have found this exercise particularly illuminating
every time that I've done it and as a result I always wake up feeling
better for it. Hopefully you will too!

CHAPTER 4

TAKING ACTION ON
THE GUIDANCE OF YOUR DREAM
THEMES AND SYMBOLS

In the previous chapter you discovered two very helpful methods of dream interpretation: *My ABC method of dream interpretation* and the *thematic method of dream interpretation*. Both of these methods show that dream work is a masterful art that, with some effort, anyone can become skilled in. Dreams are the liminal place where our humanity and divinity meet, which means that the guidance we receive in our sleep is sacred.

Ultimately, once you decode your dream message you need to put that guidance to good use by taking action in your life. So that is exactly what we are going to now focus on: the action part of your personal growth in relation to the dream messages that you receive.

Now, if I asked you to tell me how you are, what would you say? Would you tell me a story of fatigue and frustration or a narrative of serenity and acceptance? In comparison, if I asked you to tell me about how you actually want to feel, what would your answer be? Perhaps calmness is your greatest aspiration at the moment. Or maybe it's more pivotal, as in a yearning for total transformation.

The latter is something that I can really relate to. I spent a large portion of my early twenties wanting to feel supported and inspired. Yet my everyday experience was far from those aspirations. Mostly I just felt overwhelmed and anxious, which meant that my life circumstances generally reflected how I felt.

Maybe you can relate to that experience? Where there is a significant gap between where you are and where you want to be, while at the same time not really having a clue as to how to change things up for the better! Perhaps the gap is ginormous for you. Or maybe it's a simple hop to the other side of greater well-being.

Whatever the case, I believe that it's useful to know that this is where dreams are most helpful. Both our daytime dreams (the big, bold visions for our lives that we discover through our heart's inner calling) and our nighttime dreams steer us positively forward. Dreams show us just how to traverse that very gap from right here to over there by dialoguing with us through evocative imagery, symbolism, and emotion.

As you will discover, regular dreamers are able to close the gap by transmuting limiting beliefs, emotions, and behaviors in their waking life on the guidance of their dreams. Lucid dreamers close the gap by actively altering the dreamscape with conscious awareness, and then by carrying through the new emotional vibration into their waking lives. Both ways work.

TAKING ACTION AND HONORING YOUR FUTURE GOALS

When I teach people how to analyze their dreams, they usually choose to use the thematic method of dream interpretation first. Usually that's because finding themes through a dream journal is both pleasurable and easy! Sometimes people will use this method but still feel somewhat unsure as to what action to take in their waking lives. In that case, it's helpful to look at your dream themes in relation to your future goals and your current level of emotional well-being.

For some people, understanding their own level of emotional well-being is an easy process that they give little thought to. However, for many people (which included me at one point) this is definitely not the case! In order to understand your current level of emotional well-being you need to be able to actually pinpoint and name how you feel. Below is a list of emotions designed to help you recognize how you feel.

☐ Nurturing, secure, peaceful, loved

☐ Creative, cheerful, fired-up, happy

☐ Energetic, excited, joyful

☐ Trusting, confident, certain

☐ Positive expectation, optimisim, eagerness

☐ Anticipation, trusting, encouraged

☐ Satisfied, serenity, acceptance, hopeful

☐ Dull, bored, indifferent

☐ Cynical, distrusting, pessimistic

☐ Thwarted, agitated, irritated, frazzled

☐ Tender, unsettled, nervous, panicked

☐ Sad, discouraged, let-down, upset

☐ Apprehensive, concerned, hesitant

☐ Afraid, anxious, frightened

☐ Bitter, blamed, resentful

☐ Deterred, unsettled, dissatisfied

☐ Hostile, angry, hurt, in pain

☐ Retaliatory, vengeful

☐ Rage, disgust, abhorrence, hate

☐ Envy, inadequacy, jealousy

☐ Ashamed, self-conscious, afraid, unworthy

☐ Fear, dread, terror

Can you spot what your current emotional baseline is? Perhaps you are sitting somewhere between enthusiastic and hopeful. Or maybe you're discouraged and anxious. Now think about the dream themes and messages that you've discovered. Do they relay a similar emotional message or are they the complete opposite of what you are currently experiencing in your life?

When I was in my twenties, I often had repetitive dreams in which I was in some form of transportation but the pathway was always disrupted or dangerous. I would be in a car and there would be an obstruction up ahead. Or I would be on a boat and the sea would be wild and choppy. Generally, my dreams felt frenetic and more often than not I woke up feeling exhausted.

At the time, in my waking life I was on a "spiritual bypassing" kick, pretending that everything was okay, when in actuality it really wasn't! I wanted to feel calm, confident, and secure. My future goals were all centered on consistently feeling that way. But in reality, there was a really large gap between where I was and where I wanted to be. Both emotionally and pragmatically speaking.

One Saturday afternoon I sat down and thematically coded my dreams. I discovered that water, transportation, and volatile dream movement was present in almost six months' worth of dream entries. Months' worth of dream themes clearly spelled it out: "You are emotionally volatile and things are going to erupt if you don't do something!"

It became glaringly obvious that I really needed to pay attention to what I was experiencing, both in my waking life and in my dreams. I came to understand that I needed to cultivate better emotional support in my life and that I needed to heal. Looking back now, it's easy to see that my dreams couldn't have been more obvious if they tried!

But at the time, I hardly ever acted on the guidance of my dreams. I journaled them and did little else with them. I partially believe that's why my dreams were repetitive for six long months. I was dealing with pervasive, entrenched issues, so my dream themes were consistently trying to get my attention in repetitive ways.

I was on a ship and the water was insanely wild. Or I'd find myself on a road with some huge issue just up ahead. Or the car's wheels would blow out. Or the doors of the car would fly open. You get the point! It was always the same kind of dream, just spun in a slightly different way. But with the same core symbolic themes: transportation, boats, water, roads, cars, and volatility—a lack of emotional containment and direction.

Repetitive dreams (and dream themes) strongly point you right to the heart of the matter. At the time I was having those dreams, I was struggling to deal with emotions that I had squashed for years. The turbulent undercurrents of the water, or the broken roads, were indicative of what I was feeling but not expressing. Things below the surface were imploding, so to speak.

Interestingly enough I was also never the driver or the sea captain.

Someone else was always in control. You could say that my unconscious beliefs and instincts were behind the wheel or at the helm. My dreams showed me the correct action to take in my life. That was through symbolically showing me what I was not actively doing (I was never in control of the transportation) and exactly what I was doing (emotionally freaking out) in the dream. This all became so obvious after I thematically coded my dreams.

In my waking life, I needed to become the driver—the sea captain—and chart a better course for myself, which included expressing how I felt. I needed to get off the road of chaos and consciously choose control. Dream themes and messages always reveal the emotional, intimate, and spiritual needs of a person. The symbolic messages of your dreams will always guide you toward the correct action—especially if you pay attention to the larger picture!

What that looked like for me was talking to a therapist and healing from difficult past events. When I started to change how I felt (by really transforming my link to the past) my dreams changed too. If I have a similar dream nowadays, I know that I am neglecting the reality of how I feel and so I immediately prioritize my emotional well-being.

In other words, I take action much faster now on the guidance of my dreams. You may also find that the longer you do dream work the clearer certain dreams become. So you only need to experience your dream once—thank goodness—to get the message!

Ultimately, all dream themes show you the truth of your energetic and emotional level of well-being. They show you exactly how to navigate uncertainty through mapping out the next correct course of action *in relation to how you pervasively feel.* If you tend to avoid, repress, or dismiss how you generally feel in your waking life, your dreams will likely compensate for this by being very in-your-face!

Meaning that the more emotionally adept you become, the more fluid your dream guidance will be. And as a result, the easier it will become to close the gap from where you are right now to where you want to be because you'll better understand what action to take.

COMMON DREAM THEMES: THE EMOTIONS THEY GENERALLY REPRESENT AND THE CORRESPONDING ACTIONS THAT THEY IMPLY

As you can imagine there are thousands of different dream themes and symbols that can be written about. What I am hoping to impart to you is not a dream dictionary of sorts but rather a clear and accurate way of understanding, and relating to, your dream guidance. The most helpful way of doing that is by offering you an analysis of common dream themes in relation to how they make you feel so that you can know exactly what action to take in order to positively move forward in your life, work, and relationships.

From my work I've also noticed that there are a range of common dream themes that span diverging genders and cultures. There is a great body of scientific research, such as the work of Dr. Patricia Garfield, who proves the universality of dream themes. I've listed a few themes below for your convenience.

Each theme has what could be described as a "positive" and a "negative" association. I don't really like these terms because even a negative association is ultimately there to assist you. If you cloud your perception with a preemptive image of its being "good" or "bad" you taint the guidance of your dream from the get-go. So don't get too caught up in labeling your dreams. Just meet them with an open mind and heart!

COMMON DREAM THEME #1: ASCENDING OR DESCENDING

One night I had a dream in which the light from a star dripped down onto my body. I know that sounds abstract and it certainly was. With dreams we enter into the nonlinear and artful realm of metaphoric imagery. We are spoken to, in soulful metaphor, in order to awaken our spirit and evoke our emotions. That is, with the full potency of imagery intended to edge us toward our center—our truest selves.

In my dream, I was standing naked in the pitch-black darkness of the night looking out onto a field. The darkness enveloped everything around me except the sky, which I felt was alive, pulsing with mystery and stillness. Then in a flicker, a star above me caught my attention.

Curious, I began to focus on the star, watching as it glistened and then moved. Shimmers of starlight then began to descend toward me. Starlit drops touched my body as I began to fall back onto the ground. I went into the earth and was shrouded in darkness. Only moments later, I arose and ascended toward the star to meet the very energy of its radiance. I woke up with a lingering feeling of euphoria.

You will discover that you will dream beyond everyday emotional turmoil and psychological projection the more you focus on becoming a masterful dreamer. When you begin to consciously accept the imaginal realm, your interior life, and your inner divinity in all aspects of your life, the clearer it will become that your dreams are more than just the residue of the day.

Your dreams show you all the ways you are, have been, and will ever be. As with the dream theme of ascending and descending, you are a cosmic interlace, which connects the physical and nonphysical. The heavenly and the earthly. The mystical and the mundane.

In dreams we can ascend or descend in multiple ways. We fly. We fall. We climb up and down steps and ladders. We go up and down in elevators and airplanes. All the while, none the wiser that our dream symbols are speaking to us about this numinous interlace.

On a concrete level this theme deals with the chambers of our psyche, pointing us in the direction of what we have psychologically buried or are overburdened with. What's at the surface of your consciousness? What do you need to excavate from the depths of your psyche? What do you need to reach for? In dreaming we reclaim these aspects of ourselves by bringing them to conscious awareness in the forefront of the mind. Ultimately, you cannot rise without knowing what you are rising from. Knowing that as you descend farther the ascent rises equally.

We've all heard the expression to "fall from grace," an innately humbling statement that shows us what happens when we disconnect from the elegance of spirit. Ascending and descending dreams act as a symbolic reminder to cultivate our own inner spirit. (You can do that in any way that feels good to you. Here are some examples: meditation, self-inquiry, assisting those less fortunate than you, etc.) The idea is to neither sit at the bottom of the pit in self-loathing or to be so grandiose that a fall from grace is inevitable, but rather trusting that when the time is perfectly right, we ascend and descend as necessary.

COMMON DREAM THEME # 2:
BEING TRAPPED OR EXPANSION

There is a primal fear associated with being trapped and to dream of being trapped will likely evoke discomfort and even terror. From dreams of being stuck in small spaces (like in the trunks of cars), to nightmares of being confined by a person or situation, being trapped is not an easy experience. If you often experience this kind of dream theme then this is a clear message to put your full force behind getting unstuck in your waking life.

It's easy to fall into the belief that you may be a victim of your circumstances. And although this may be the case in your waking life (for example, if you've been a victim of trauma or violence) in your dream life it is not the case. In your dream life it is a call to reclaim your ability to respond to your environment, your relationships, and, most importantly, how you feel. Your dreams, and spirit, will always support you in finding ways to explore creative freedom and well-being.

Sometimes the only way out is through radical acceptance of where you currently are: a space that feels so suffocating in its experience that you will do *anything* to crawl out of its confines. In other words, to use your inner power to expand beyond the limitations in which you find yourself in order to find the freedom that you need!

If we also look to the various words we can use to describe being trapped, this is what comes up: confinement, imprisonment, entombment, surrounded, and stuck. Depending on the other dream symbols and themes that you experience, you will know which word is most appropriate for your experience.

For example, a dream of being buried alive is thematically clear in meaning: the violent death of something still alive. This can be a psychological instinct, a relationship, inner spirit, a feeling, a goal, a wish, or more dauntingly a representation of a part of the personality that has been buried.

The dream then comes to alert the dreamer to self-guard their most intimate desires until they are more fully formed. Or to mourn the loss of something dearly held that was abruptly taken away and as always, the other dream symbols will illuminate what action needs to be taken.

So, one way or another, dreams of being trapped are a message to empower yourself in whatever way that you can. Even just one small step will help! A helpful antidote to feeling trapped is simply to begin to use your voice. Speak to what makes you feel trapped and in doing so name the confines of entrapment. Follow through by declaring, out loud, what you would prefer to experience and then follow through by taking action.

On the flip side of being trapped is the experience of expansion, ease, and freedom. Dreams of beaches, playfulness, and footloose wonder, expansion dreams feel good to dream. I know I'm in a state of emotional expansion when I spontaneously dream of traveling through foreign countries. I love to explore, so expansion in dreams just feels wonderful.

Sometimes these dreams come out of the blue and at other times they are so obviously related to where you find yourself. Both usually carry a message of timing: the one to nurture the feeling of expansion in your everyday life and to trust that future expansion is possible for you, no matter your current circumstances, and the other a clear sign that whatever you're doing in your waking life is working or soon will take off—so keep going!

The dream theme of expansion can also show the ways in which you are released from some form of difficulty or confining scenario. That is because the theme of expansion can be felt and represented symbolically on a spectrum. For example, having dreams in which chains are being broken, or discovering new rooms and doorways. No matter the dream, the action is clear: break free from limitations and open the door to expansion.

COMMON DREAM THEME #3: BEING CHASED OR EMBRACED

I cannot tell you how many people I have worked with who have experienced repetitive dreams in which they are being chased. Sometimes being chased is simply an upsetting representation of a certain level of anxiety that follows through into your nighttime dreams. If that resonates with you, I highly recommend Arianna Huffington's book *The Sleep Revolution: Transforming Your Life, One Night at a Time*, for sleep practices that help.

But being chased in a dream is often symbolically representative of much more than just anxiety. If you, like many other people, have repetitively dreamed of being chased, it may be time to look at how you *really* feel and who you believe yourself to be. You may believe that in order to maintain the status quo in your life, you need to behave or be seen in a certain way. When you are being chased, your dreams are really trying to tell you that you can't outrun yourself, the past, or your future!

In these types of dreams, it's helpful to note what or who is chasing you because this can be an illuminating insight for you. Are you chased by men or women? Are animals tailing you? Or are there numerous people (like a group of soldiers) hunting you down? Or is it just one ambivalent or scary figure? (We'll fully explore dream figures later on; this is just to show you how to reflect more broadly in relation to your common dream themes.)

If the "thing" that was chasing you caught you, what do you think would happen? And on the flipside of that, what do you think would happen if you willingly turned to face the persecutor of your dreams? That is, with the full force of your emotional strength, power, and even love?

On the other end of the spectrum of being chased are the lovely sorts of dreams in which you are embraced. Being embraced in your dreams can be a call to be more compassionate with yourself and other people. Or it can signal a yearning for more intimacy, connection, and love in all of its forms (romantic, sexual, or platonic). As a thematic marker it calls to you to look at the ways in which your life currently nurtures and embraces you. And to then take appropriate action to embrace all the goodness that life has to offer you.

COMMON DREAM THEME #4:
DEATH, LIFE, AND REBIRTH

The death/life/rebirth theme in dreams is primordial in nature and I would probably need to write an entire book on this theme to really do it justice. What I will say is that you need to first identify how you feel about death and dying, as well as life and rebirth, before you begin to fully dive into these dream themes. Once you know how you personally relate to these themes, the manner in which they are presented to you in your dreams will begin to make much more sense.

The death/life dream theme has to do with beginnings, endings, transformation, and growth. Look at how you are relating to the cycles in your life. Both death and birth are an initiation. A rite of passage. Right now, ask yourself: What situation, process, person, or circumstance is initiating me?

Self-reflective questions always help you in your process of dream interpretation and personal growth inquiry. Learn to feel for the right questions. Then look to see how you are interacting with these questions and themes in both your dreams and your life.

Perhaps you are holding on to something that is dead or rotten (corpse dreams). Or are you breathing life into something new? Is the baby in the dream you, full of potential but vulnerable? Are you mourning at a wedding and celebrating at a funeral? What cycle of change is gusting through? Are you in a field of flowers in full bloom?

What is dying away? What is being birthed? Do you look like an older or younger "you" in the dream? Do you dream of all things strange that go bump in the night? All are symbolic of the cosmic interplay between life and death and housed in the experience of your dreams.

Rebirth, on the other hand, encompasses both life and death. It is a representative phoenix that rises from the ashes. It is burnt, dead, dust. Seemingly over and without hope—that is, until it rises. It transforms through the very dirt of death to once again breathe in life. Fully embodying both death and life in a beautiful circle of rebirth.

Death, birth, and rebirth are forces that are larger than us. Yet they are also channeled and experienced through us. They signify the mystery that animates all life. That's why there is always an implicit level of surrender present in this dream message and theme. And as with any initiation, when you fully surrender to the process you move through it to reach the other side, and are never quite the same as before.

HOW TO UNDERSTAND YOUR PERSONAL ASSOCIATION TO COLLECTIVE SYMBOLS AND DREAM THEMES

Dream themes and symbols have a proclivity to evoke emotion in a similar way among many different people. We all know what it feels like to be chased, but who is doing the chasing is what is unique to each and every one of us. By the same token, we can all reflect on the collective dream theme of nurturance.

We can dream many different images of what nurturance is. Corn, food, and mother are just three such symbolic images. All three are rooted in the greater embodied experience of what it means to be filled with substance and love. *To be nurtured.*

Yet perhaps the "corn of fulfillment" never came to sustain you and so you have been left feeling famished for longer than you can remember. How then would you start to nurture yourself if your very own caregiver never knew how? You begin by feeding the hunger that it represents within your inner world.

When you work with imagery and symbols it is helpful to look both at the collective (or common) meanings as well as your own personal experiences with said image or symbol. Just as "mother" is a collective symbol that holds many connotations, it will, at the same time, represent something completely unique to you. Flowers are another wonderful example of a collective symbol. Throughout the world, different cultures use flowers to honor important events or rites of passage in life such as weddings, birthdays, anniversaries, funerals. Flowers in their innate structure are universally representative of three cycles: being seeded, blooming, and wilting. (We see this cycle so clearly in the natural process of aging.) If we look even closer we can see that flowers also symbolically represent the larger motif of death, life, and rebirth.

So if you dream of flowers, look to see what kind they are, as well as what physical condition they were in to garner your dream guidance. My own dream experience with flowers follows:

My sister absolutely loves jasmine flowers. She's loved them since she was a little girl. In fact, we would walk around the neighborhood together and she would always stop to gather them. Something she still loves to do to this very day! Every time I see jasmine flowers I am reminded of her and I am flooded with good memories and emotions.

So when I dream of a jasmine flower I know that it is a particularly unique symbol for me. Steeped in rich imagery and emotion, it reminds me of what it means to have a loving and sisterly relationship. Jasmine flowers are both uniquely symbolic for me but collective in representation. A dream that signifies my personal association to a collective dream symbol follows:

I was happily standing in a wide-open field when suddenly, without warning, I began to become entrapped by jasmine vines. The vines began to move up my body, eventually encircling my throat and slowly suffocating me. Even though I felt scared, I somehow managed to declare that I no longer wanted to be entwined with the jasmine vines. And in that moment the flowers released their grip on me. The vines then unrooted themselves and moved to the bottom of the field, far away from me.

In my waking life, at the time of that dream, I was in a toxic friendship but I hadn't wanted to face the truth of the situation. The relationship was the very opposite of a sisterly companionship. In my dream I was shown the state of my denial and how continuing the friendship was harming me. I realized that I needed to voice my truth and exit the relationship (a symbolic death) in order to afford us both the opportunity to bloom elsewhere (a symbolic rebirth).

You too will find that in your dreams you will experience symbols and dream themes that are more charged with meaning for you, simply because you have memories associated with them. In those times, it's important to use your own experiences to understand why you are seeing that symbol in that specific way and in that exact moment of your life. And if you are still in doubt, lean into my golden question of dream interpretation by asking: Why this dream, in this way, at this time?

CHAPTER 5

TRAVERSING COMMON
SYMBOLIC DREAMSCAPES

A s dreamers we travel through the dreamscapes of the Underworld, the Inner World, and the Outer World. The Underworld: a mirror to the unconscious. The Inner World: the landscape of your heart and soul. The intrinsic connection you have to spirit. As well as the liminal realm of unlimited possibilities that lucid dreamers become intimately acquainted with. The Outer World: the dream reflection of the material world that we call life or reality. All three "worlds" indicated and represented by the actual dreamscape and by the movement we take within the dream.

In dreamscapes we can find ourselves in houses, buildings, offices, malls, parking lots, forests, mountains, caves, deserts, forests, gardens, bodies of water, and even different countries. Sometimes these places are well known to us and at other times they are entirely foreign. At times we move through these places frenetically and at others more stably and peacefully. And so, with dreamscape imagery *we look to move in the direction of wholeness and balance in relation to where we find ourselves and what we see and do as a result.*

Dream places can illuminate the state of your personal life and also the state of the collective. By the collective I mean nature, life, and the state of all people on the planet. In other words, the greater whole. Below, you'll discover the most common dreamscapes that I hear about from my workshop participants and clients. It is my recommendation that you work with your dreamscapes with the intention of harmonizing any discordant elements found within the dream. Let's journey together through the multitude of these symbolic dream places.

#1: A CAVE: A MULTI- SYMBOLIC DREAMSCAPE THAT INITIATES THE DREAMER THROUGH THE PROCESS OF GOING INWARD

Throughout history caves have held significance for human beings. They have been used as burial chambers, spaces of primal safety and shelter, and places of sacred worship and connection. The rock art found in caves all over the world is testament to an ancient and sacred communion that spans many different cultures.

Caves have evoked a multitude of symbolic meanings due to their historical and spiritual use. A cave in myth or legend often speaks to the Divine Feminine. It is seen to be a cosmic womb where the person who ventures into it is initiated and who upon exiting is reborn in some sense. Caves are places associated with the death/life/rebirth theme but they also innately signify the primal necessity of shelter and safety. Caves can be healing places or spaces of terror, all depending on the dreamer's story.

We need only look at myth to further see the collective truth found in this pivotal dreamscape. Following the Japanese Shinto religion and the story of the sun goddess Amaterasu we come to learn the power of the cave. Her story is as follows:

The beautiful sun goddess desperately retreated into a cave after her younger brother terrorized her through a number of cruel actions. When she withdrew into the cave, she took her light with her and the world was plunged into darkness. Naturally, chaos ensued, resulting in eight hundred gods congregating outside of the cave in an attempt to coax her out. You see, they, and the world, so desperately needed her light.

It was only when the celestial goddess Amenouzume decided to transform the situation with laughter that things started to turn around. She danced wildly outside the cave while at the same time flashing different parts of her naked body to the crowd. The result was an absolute uproar of laughter from the gods.

The sun goddess, curious about the laughter, then peeked outside the cave. Instead of seeing the commotion she saw her own reflection in a mirror that had been purposefully placed outside the cave. In that very moment, she was reminded of her own innate divinity and beauty. And with that she stepped out of the cave and the world was once again steeped in light.

Caves are never particularly well lit and so the darkness that encompasses the cave is intrinsic to its meaning. The darkness is fruitful. Caves are not necessarily spaces that we psychologically associate with freedom. Rather, the cave as a collective symbol is a place where we retreat, survive, enter, commune, or seek vision. They are the dark treasure troves of inward incubation.

Caves are physical, natural places of containment. But the containment is as individualized as the actual cave and the person entering it. The cave will be a safe space or place of entrapment depending on you, the dreamer, and where you currently find yourself in the terrain of your life.

Many of the dreamers that I have worked with will dream of caves when they are in a process of great inner transition or transformation (moving houses, life stages, jobs, divorce, etc.). When they are actively immersed in their spiritual journeys and are about to, or need to, rediscover their own inner will to live.

People will often dream of caves when they are being initiated into a new cycle that requires resilience and courage. This could be a journey of becoming a first-time mother or father. Or after a bereavement process that influences the inner world of the griever. (This is when it's perhaps helpful to look to the story of Amaterasu and remember that laughter has the power to soften grief.)

If you dream of a cave it's important to look at how you felt during your time spent there. Did you venture into the cave? Were you chased into the cave in the dream? Was the entrance/exit visible? Did you have a light with you or did you find one? Was the cave in darkness? How did you feel in the dream? What was the whole dream and how did the cave fit into what you were experiencing?

As with any dream landscape, your attitude toward its symbolism both in your dream and in your waking life is what will offer further insight into the dream's meaning. If you are lucid dreaming and enter into a cave, ask it to tell you its story—you're likely in for quite a tale! Or alternatively simply explore the cave as you see fit.

Alternative dream symbols associated with the cave: tent, grotto, or labyrinth.

#2: A MOUNTAIN: A DREAMSCAPE OF STRENGTH AND ENDURANCE

There are many ways that a dreamer can interact with a mountain. If you dream that you are about to reach a summit and are looking ahead at the vast horizon, you will likely feel a catharsis of sorts. You'll feel the overwhelming bliss of contentment that comes from achieving hard things. From success well earned. A summit dream often symbolically represents a significant achievement that the dreamer will soon experience in their waking life or has recently achieved.

If you are struggling to climb the mountain, you need to question where you are going in your life and why. What's your underlying motivation? Are you going to give up or continue? Do you need to muster the inner strength to go the distance?

Oftentimes I hear of dreams wherein the dreamer is driving on a mountain, navigating sharp turns and steep cliffs. The dreamer is in control of the car but the drive feels intense. It's adrenaline-inducing dream imagery to know that with one wrong turn of the wheel it's a plummet to the ground! On the surface these kinds of dreams may appear negative, but that's generally not the case.

These kinds of dreams simply signal the process of metamorphosis that the dreamer is undergoing. It takes a great deal of inner courage to make significant changes in life. So a mountain dream gives a symbolic voice to the journey that the dreamer is on. The dream is an internal acknowledgment of the transformation that is occurring.

When you are in a process of emotional or psychological transformation, the changes required to succeed can often feel overwhelming and even emotionally threatening. Especially if you are abandoning a long-standing pattern of behavior. For instance, if you are addicted to something (or someone) and you then seriously (like bone deep) commit to changing your ways, you may have a mountain dream in which a steep cliff is the focal point.

The stakes, like the sheer drop, are high if you abandon your well-being again. So your dreams send you a message through the mountain—and the car, and the sheer drop—to alert you of your need for courage. To make you aware of the leap in consciousness required to experience something better. Your dream comes to you to remind you to not give up! So that you will choose better on a daily basis in order to feel better.

I've had many clients who, when working on ancestral limits, will also have these kinds of dreams. An ancestral limit is a problem or issue that your lineage (for the most part) has grappled with. For example, a repeated pattern of failed marriages within a family history would be considered an ancestral limit. Whether from divorce, substance abuse, mental illness, or other barriers to a successful marriage, the pattern of failed unions throughout generations can be traced. Ancestral limits often speak to intergenerational trauma—trauma passed down from one generation to the next.

Think about your own family. Can you see how, somehow, people often or always seem to end up in the same kinds of scenarios or situations? If the answer is yes, then you're likely dealing with an inherited pattern of belief. This may now be up to you to bust!

Sometimes a family, going back generations, is severely stuck in one way of doing or being. There may have been limits or obstacles that prevented the lineage from changing or adapting. That is, until the dreamer's life. So the dreamer is conquering the mountain and in doing so is changing something that their entire lineage could not accomplish. What a journey!

Perhaps your grandparents set camp at the base of the mountain and then your parents stagnated mid-mountain. So now, here you are, driving (not walking!) up the mountain. Your dream is telling you to go further than your lineage could and to keep your vision set on the path ahead.

It takes a lot of strength and determination to climb an actual mountain and it takes even more endurance to climb a metaphoric mountain. It is anxiety provoking to go where you haven't gone before and to willingly step into the unknown. But that doesn't mean you can't, or that you should give up! In fact, your dreams say otherwise. Embrace your feelings of anxiety but continue to climb, continue to move forward.

When you dream of a mountain you're on a journey of spiritual endurance. You don't need a map because your dreams are the GPS (great presenting symbols) guiding you all the way. There are no errors in your dreams and how you receive them. Even if you would prefer to dream of more pleasant things, sometimes you simply *need* a mountain type of dream.

A mountain dreamscape can also symbolize different versions of the Self and also different periods of time. The base of the mountain may represent the past version of youself and your literal history. The middle of the mountain may represent the present moment and who you see yourself to be right now. The peak of the mountain may represent your highest, most actualized Self that will be experienced in the future.

Mountain dreams can resolve themselves. Sometimes that happens in the dream (particularly if the dreamer doesn't wake up from the anxiety of the dream). At other times, it can happen through a series of repetitive dreams that are slightly different each time. This is usually due to what's actually happening in the dreamer's waking life and the steps that they are actively taking to conquer the metaphoric mountain. Either way it is always possible for the dreamer to get to the top of the mountain, both in life and in their dreams.

Modern-day equivalents of a mountain: skyscrapers, a tower or a high-rise, and elevators are often linked to this dreamscape.

#3: OPEN FIELDS AS A DREAMSCAPE: SIGNIFYING EXPANSIVE POSSIBILITIES

If you find yourself in an open and vast landscape in your dreams, it means that the answers you are seeking are in plain sight—there are no visual obstructions. A field is a place full of emotion. Many people dream of open fields when they need to explore alternative options to the circumstances they find themselves in. Fields represent an abundance of opportunities that the dreamer needs to rediscover by simply looking around. The field is a rich metaphoric ground where solutions can be sought and found.

If you find yourself in a situation in your waking life where it seems like there is *only* one way forward or just one answer, then a field of dreams will remind you that you're too close to the situation and that you need to step out and seek assistance. Or alternatively you may simply need to broaden your view.

A field's meaning is experienced through the emotion it evokes within you during your dream. Where were you standing in the field, on the periphery or in the center? If you were on the edge, ask yourself: Am I on the edge of possibility? If you found yourself walking through an overgrown field, ask yourself: What needs clearing in my life? Perhaps you've already stepped into a way of living that resonates with infinite possibilities and are seeing confirmation of that through your nighttime dreams.

Modern-day equivalents of a field: sports fields, parks, botanical gardens, golf courses.

#4: A HOUSE: A DREAMSCAPE OF EMOTIONAL LOVE, BOUNDARIES, AND PRIMAL SAFETY

A house in a dream is once again a collective symbol with great personal meaning. In psychological terms, a house, as a dream symbol, represents the state of the dreamer's psyche. But it can also speak to the state of health of the dreamer's body (as can vehicles). That said, not all houses make a home.

When we use the word "home" we mean it to encompass so much more than just physical stability and security. A home is a place ideally filled with love, connection, and warmth. It is a place filled with nurturance, comfort, and safety. It is a sacred space: a place in the world that is uniquely yours and that shelters you from external forces. The "four walls" of a home represent the clear boundary between you and the outside world.

As we dream we are re-creating our memories, not just in relation to our history but also in service to where we currently find ourselves. If you grew up in a place that housed difficult experiences then you will need to tend to your inner house (your psyche) so that you can move forward unencumbered in your life.

You can learn to house new experiences and your dreams will guide you on that journey, as you've seen throughout the course of this book. Your psyche can become an inner sanctum where you experience love, safety, and well-being, which you can then move forward into your relationships.

If you dream of transient homes like hotels or motels, ask yourself: Am I finding temporary shelter in a person, place, or thing, and how do I feel about this? Your emotional response to the dreamscape will offer insight as to whether your choices in your waking life are helping or hindering you. Of course, if you have a strong affinity and love for hotels and you dream of one, it is likely that your dream is a message of comfort, relaxation, and even luxury, as opposed to a message of feeling displaced.

Again, your personal associations with collective dream symbols will influence the meaning of your dream messages. The broader symbolism of a house speaks to the containment of emotions, beliefs, and experiences found within the dreamer. Houses signify primal or foundational matters and will reflect the dreamer's relationship to such matters by, for example, the actual look of the house. Is the house in shambles, in good order, or lavish beyond belief?

Other forms of "houses" are hospitals, libraries, malls, schools, and churches. The hospital is a house of healing. The library is a storehouse of knowledge. A school a house of learning. The mall, a house of procurement. A church a house of worship. Once again, look to self-reflective and open-ended questions to illuminate your dream messages further by exploring what you were doing in the dream and how you felt along the way.

You might ask: What is this place teaching me? How is this place different from what I know and have actually experienced? Or alternatively: How is this dreamscape similar to what I know? Most importantly, did a new dreamscape offer you a new experience, such as living in a charmed castle? If so, then how can you take action to experience or invite that feeling into your waking life?

Alternative dream symbols for a house: temple, castle, hotel, B&B, or motel.

#5 WATER: A DREAMSCAPE EMBODYING EMOTIONS, THE UNCONSCIOUS, THE SOUL, AND PSYCHIC MATTERS

Have you ever seen a puddle of water that has gotten cut off from the rest of the stream? It stagnates and quite literally begins to stink. Water needs movement and flow in order to stay healthy. This is the same thing when it comes to your emotions. If you block off how you feel or let things fester below the surface, your emotions putrefy. In response, your dreams will get the emotional flow moving once again in order to counterbalance what you are doing or experiencing in your waking life.

You'll dream of a kettle boiling over (emotional anger) or a bursting geyser (needing to cry). You'll dream of going under in wild waters (volatile emotions or people that overwhelm you) or having uninvited guests in your shower (uneasy vulnerability). Your dreams will do whatever it takes to get your intrapsychic life flowing once again!

At its essence water speaks to our life force. It's what nourishes us and keeps as alive. Rain may fall in your dreams and cleanse a situation that you are dealing with. You might find yourself swimming with dolphins in pure enjoyment or running a soothing bath. Perhaps a dream figure offers you a liquid elixir of total bliss and well-being. At all times the water is awakening something primal within you. That is confirmation of your innate ability to flow with life and meander through all the emotional terrains of your life.

Water symbolizes so much more than just our emotions. It speaks to the theme of creation and destruction. One need only think of an oasis or a tsunami to understand the power that it holds.

Water is the chalice of receptivity seen as liquid femininity. It can shift into three different forms depending on the conditions around it: steam, frozen, or flowing. In your dreams you will interact with all three states. Look to see how these states mimic your actions or emotions in waking life.

Alternative dream symbols for water: rain, pool, lake, dam, jacuzzi, waterfall, ocean, sea, cenote.

NAVIGATING YOUR DREAMSCAPE

In waking life we usually have to use some mode of transportation to get where we want to go. Yet, in dreams we often just flash from one dream scene to the next. If you can recognize that you just appeared somewhere in a dream, that recognition can in turn trigger lucidity. Most people dream of multiple places during one night, so there are plenty of opportunities to become conscious in your dreams! It's helpful to recognize how you get to places in any kind of dream because it relates to your personal growth. It shows you how to navigate change more gracefully between different elements in your life.

Scroll back through your dream journal to see how many times you suddenly appear elsewhere in your dreams. Look to see if the junctures where you transit to another dreamscape are thematically repetitive. These junctures are highly personalized and as such are unique to you. For example, do you change dream scenes every time you feel a specific way or when a specific type of dream figure appears? Perhaps you're in a house, which is always then followed by being at a beach?

The junctures of the dreamscapes are asking you to look at them holistically in order to garner insight. I liken this dream experience to reading a story or watching a movie that has parallel stories woven within a larger narrative, all of which usually come together at the end. Like snippets of chapters all relating to one story, or soul, that encompasses a larger journey. Junctures in dreamscapes help us to see the bigger picture and how it all ties in together.

It's also helpful to recognize how you get to places in your dreams because the actual mode of transportation is symbolically rich in meaning too. You might find yourself walking, driving, or commuting in a subway, ship, train, or taxi. All are forms of transportation, with singular differences, that are hinged on the collective image of movement.

Look at means of transport and the level of comfort within the mode of transport. Is it fancy, futuristic, olden-day, regular, or broken? Is the transportation communal and are there other travelers with you? Singular modes of transportation speak to a journey that you embark on alone. Collective modes of transport can signify your place within your community or how you feel regarding the group or people you surround yourself with.

Common sense is also helpful here. Say, for example, you always take the subway and then you begin to see subways in your dreams—this might just be speaking to your everyday normalcy. Use your own judgment to feel for what is accurate. My guidelines are just that—guidelines—not absolutes!

Trains are wonderfully illuminating dream symbols. They are held on tracks and move in one direction (does that sound like you, your beliefs, or your life?). They can go under and over land, as well as through tunnels and checkpoints. Trains have conductors who are safety guardians of the passengers; engineers steer the way forward. Old trains let off steam—a very on-the-nose message telling the dreamer to release tension or anger.

Ships, on the other hand, traverse water, which means that you're traveling on the surface of what is emotionally occurring inside you. Is the water choppy, rough, or calmly azure? In other words, how are you *really* feeling? Much like my dream of needing to become the captain of my own life, are you making the decisions in your life or are you allowing, or hoping, someone else will take control? Are you under the influence of unruly instincts and beliefs?

Modes of transport show us how we adapt to circumstances thrust upon us and as a result what best action to take in our waking life. Look to see whether you are moving upward or downward (ascending or descending); journeying through a spiral (cyclical patterns or cycles); or stuck somewhere in the middle.

Modes of transport, and the movement they speak to, show you just how you are navigating as you travel through this emotional and spiritual journey that is life. And remember, if you're not enjoying the ride, get off the damn bus and choose a different road!

EXERCISE #1: ENVISIONING SPECIFIC DREAM PLACES FOR GREATER WELL-BEING

You are the temple. You are the house. You are the cave. You are the mountain. With all places you are welcomed back to discover a facet of who you are. You walk through old childhood places and discover new dream places so that you can reignite your inspiration and embody your spiritual greatness.

You may find it helpful to meditate on specific dreamscapes in your waking life so that you can reclaim what feels good. For example, if you've been feeling tired and depleted, you can meditate on a dreamscape that feels invigorating to you. It could be a vision of a waterfall that you step into, allowing the water to wash over you and soothe your senses. Or it could be a vision of you lying in a beautiful meadow with the wind breezing gently over you.

The idea with this exercise is to embody the experience fully. You don't look to analyze or decode your inner vision. You simply move with it and allow it to shape you. I have found that most of my workshop participants find this exercise particularly soothing and illuminating. Your imagination can and will guide you wonderfully if you simply allow it to. The more you do this, the easier it will also become to use your inner vision. The trick is to participate fully in the process and not to cloud it with any intellectual, egoic, or judgmental thoughts.

EXERCISE #2: DREAMING WITH YOUR DREAMSCAPES

You may find that simply through decoding your dream messages you have worked with your dreamscapes enough. However, if you would like to further explore your Inner World you can do the following exercise for greater insight. If you are a lucid dreamer you can do this exercise in the dream. Simply follow the same process.

Take a couple of deep breaths in and out to center yourself. Then close your eyes and picture a dreamscape. Let what naturally arises come to mind and allow it to play out. Try to not influence the imaginal process. Simply suspend your rational thoughts if you can and just observe the imagery that arises.

This process is usually very quick (anywhere from thirty seconds to three minutes). When you're finished, open your eyes and stretch out your body. Then when you are ready, recall the first image that popped into your mind. That is the image that you should begin to work with. It is often the most accurate and telling image of what you need to know delivered from the depths of your inner being. You can then use the ABC method of interpretation to discover its message.

EXERCISE #3: IMAGINAL RECONSTRUCTION WITH REGULAR DREAMS

This exercise is designed to help you incorporate all the seemingly emotionally dissonant notes of your dreams into a new and greater vision for your life. Before you begin this exercise choose *one* repetitive dream theme that you want to work with. You can deliberately choose a dream theme that relates to your future goals and emotional well-being; alternatively, you can spontaneously decide which theme to work with based on how you feel. You should do this exercise during a time and in a place where you will not be disturbed.

Once you are ready, find a comfortable seated position or lie down to begin the visualization. In your mind's eye imagine a scenario in which the dream theme appears very prominently. You can either replay a dream that you've actually had or re-create one entirely. The core ingredient you need to fulfill this exercise is simply the dream theme.

Try to imagine the dream theme and experience as powerfully as you can. Only when the dream theme is highly present and palpable should you begin to actively change the visualization by imagining a positive and brilliant ending. You can make the visualization as realistic or fantastical as you want. The idea is to let the images arise organically but to steer them in the direction of your choosing.

For example, if being trapped is one of your repetitive dreams or dream themes, you would imagine a scenario in which you are trapped. You would allow yourself to feel the discomfort that being trapped brings and then you would visualize a best-case scenario happening that turns the whole dream vision around. Perhaps you are trapped in an anxiety-provoking, claustrophobia-inducing tiny space in the basement of your house. You panic, but then suddenly you remember that you've got a pocketknife with you! You jimmy the door lock and it clicks open. You swing the door open with the full might of your force and you are free!

Then you walk up the stairs and exit the house. As you step outside you breathe in the fresh air and feel the sunlight on your face. You see a wide-open field of blooming roses. You walk through the roses and their innate beauty clears away any lingering feeling of being overwhelmed. Then in a moment of brilliant inspiration, you decide to buy the house so that you can remodel the entire space—specifically the room that you were trapped in!

You see the house being torn down and in its place a beautiful Japanese-inspired house appears. You walk through all of the traditionally small spaces of the house (the closet, the pantry, the basement) and you realize that they are now all super-sized sun-filled rooms boasting the essence of Zen. Bliss! Without a shadow of a doubt, you now know that you cannot ever be trapped in the house because it is designed to your very liking. You are ecstatic that things turned out so well for you!

The goal of this exercise is to repair the dream in your waking life through the use of your imagination. Your waking imagination has an active influence on your unconscious processes, emotions, and psychological instincts. By practicing this exercise you exert an outside influence onto your inward processes for the better. As a result, your repetitive dream themes are likely to change because you have altered your psychological landscape.

CHAPTER 6

✳

OPENING UP TO YOUR
DREAM FIGURES

Have you ever had a moment in your life, or in dreams, where it felt like all the windows in your mind were finally opened to let in fresh air? A *whoosh of liberating inspiration* that moves through you in one swift movement. That electric feeling is what instant alignment with your inner being or the Self feels like. In spiritual self-help the lingo used to explain the Self is often ascribed to coming into contact with the Highest Self; the Inner Being; the divinity within; the spark of God. When you are in touch with your Highest Self you feel alive, inspired, and at ease—all at the same time.

This connection to your Highest Self is also why metaphysical teachers, or dream teachers, will always teach you to use your will, interpretation, and intention in a good and correct way. That is, to tell the dream story (and your waking life narrative) in a potent way, one that is in a manner of well-being and benevolence on the guidance of the soul through that very spark of Inner Divinity. Rather than through the small lens of egoic desires, which can often verge on being grandiose or diminutive.

We have the tendency as humans to get stuck in mindsets, problems, or relationships that aren't working out for us. It's so easy to become entrenched in one way of thinking and feeling, specifically about ourselves and the world around us. To be stuck in seeing life through a limited and skewed lens. So our dreams come to re-awaken our soulful perspective through nightly storytelling and the dream figures that appear within them.

There are generally three schools of thought regarding what and who dream figures are. They are as follows:

1. Dream figures are psychological projections of your own mind, all of whom represent different aspects of your psyche. This can include shadow figures, which can be a reflection of your unconscious impulses, beliefs, emotions, and drives. They're the stuff nightmares are usually made of!

2. All dream figures are simply figments of your imagination.

3. Dream figures are part of a nonphysical essence and as such can be sentient.

I work with the first and third schools of thought. I don't believe that dream figures are simply forms of imagination. That is because of my firsthand lucid dream experiences and from the insight I've gained from regular dreams, which is simply too profound for that to be true. I'm sure that you will make up your own mind as you explore more of your own dream experiences.

The dream figures that you meet can often inform aspects of yourself, your story, and the experiences that you are having in your everyday life. For example, a dream that features a persistent or overbearing dream figure can highlight the equivalent behavior, or set of beliefs held, in waking life. In many ways, this is the psychological and intuitive insight work that you do when you interpret your dreams. You look to see how the dream *as a whole*—the dream places, symbols, figures, and actions—gives you a message of guidance through the interaction of the sum of all the parts.

As we reconnect nightly with our spiritual essence we can also dream of loved ones or dream figures who guide us positively forward. Or other spiritual guides who offer us support, comfort, and peace at times of distress or crisis. These kinds of dream figures are differentiated through the emotional force that they impart to you.

But how do you know when a dream figure is of a more numinous nature or simply a projection of your own mind and psychology?

If you can lucid dream, you can also ask these dream figures to give you information that can verify them. My experience of it, as well as that of many other people, shows that it is the feeling that these figures leave you with, that awakens something deep within you that knows that it is true and real. It's the same feeling of resonance no matter what kind of dream it is, whether regular or lucid. These dream experiences are also generally (not always) followed through with some form of synchronicity or "proof" in waking life.

This was certainly the case for my mother, who had a pivotal dream when she was in her thirties. At the time of her dream, in her waking life, she was already married and had been for about five or six years.

In her dream she was standing in a wide-open field. Then, as is the way in dreams, with no particular destination in mind she began to walk toward a hill up ahead. She walked up the hill and when she reached the top she was suddenly enrobed in a wedding dress. A sense of serenity and peace washed over her as she saw her father far away in the distance. They waved to each other. Moments later she woke up.

A few weeks later her father died unexpectedly.

Her dream was rich with symbolism and prophetic in nature. In the dream my mother is in a wide-open field (the place of possibilities) and sees a hill. Just like a mountain, the hill here is symbolic of spiritual strength and a higher vantage point. In the dream she walks toward the hill and begins to climb it. (Do you recognize the ascension theme present once again?)

Once she reaches the top of the hill she realizes that she is wearing a wedding dress. The wedding dress is a symbol of a union, as well as a marker of life cycles and stages of initiation. It shows us that the union, the marriage, is of a spiritual nature. (We know this through the interaction between the two dream symbols: the wedding dress and the peak of the hill.)

She felt serene looking at her father (a comforting dream experience that also mirrored their loving relationship in waking life). Fathers give away brides at weddings, and I can't help but think that in this dream she was "giving him away," or back to spirit. They waved to each other.

She woke up and couldn't shake the feeling that her dream was important. In the weeks following her father's death she was greatly comforted by that dream. Especially because she did not have the chance to say goodbye to him before he passed. The dream offered her a form of closure, one that she would need in order to endure the months of mourning his unanticipated death.

Although not all of our dreams are prophetic in nature, there is a certain level of emotional gravity to the dream when it is prophetic. This is reflected in the dream experience of one of my friends:

In her dream she is back at her old high school. Her teacher is writing something on the blackboard but she's struggling to read what it says. The teacher notices this and tells her to write "vitamin B12" in her notebook. She wakes up and manages to recall the dream.

In her waking life, my friend had been incredibly fatigued. The dream triggered her to take action and check out her vitamin B12 levels. She discovered that she was in fact B12 deficient and that her fatigue was likely a result of it.

When I asked her why she took action on the dream, she told me that the teacher in the dream was someone who, in her waking life, she had greatly appreciated and respected when she was in high school. She had helped her above and beyond everyday school issues. She figured that if her teacher had something to say to her now, it was likely important and she should listen!

We could say that the dream figure here, her beloved teacher, was a part of her psyche alerting her to an imbalance in her health in a symbolic way that she would understand and listen to. Her dream, as you can see, proved highly beneficial in her waking life because it helped her to become healthier and more vibrant.

All dream figures' actions inform part of the dream message. If a much-loved person shows up in your dreams, then pay attention to what they did, showed you, or said to you. Think about how you feel about them in your waking life and then link the dream. If, say, a person shouts at you in a dream and this behavior is contrary to the way they usually act in your waking life, ask yourself what situation would cause them to do such a thing?

Pay attention to all of your dream clues. They may be shouting at you because you've been avoiding red flags in your waking life. Or they may be yelling at you to show you what you need to do to let out your rage. That you need to shout and scream or, conversely, that you are doing that too much! They may be shouting at you so that you don't give up on your heart's dreams, when something challenging has left you doubting yourself. The clues are there to push you forward so that you may persevere and win.

Dream figures often appear as people that we trust. Our bond with them allows us to listen to them—to trust the message they are trying to send. The dream message speaks to well-being even if, at first, the actions seem strange or off-kilter.

But if your dream figures can offer such great insight, what does it mean if the dream figure is frightening or horrible?

Difficult dream figures can represent parts of you that you are denying or aspects of your psyche that you are not in conscious contact with. These can be aspects of your personality, unconscious motivators, past experiences, and even difficult or repressed emotions that you need to come to terms with. The following dream illustrates this:

In the dream, the dreamer finds herself at an event. (The occasion is unknown to the dreamer.) The place is busy and she feels at ease as she walks through the crowd. The dreamer nods to many of the guests that she recognizes and knows. She walks toward the front-row seating and notices that there is a stage.

She finds a prime seat and is eagerly awaiting the honorary speaker. But instead of the honorary speaker, an unexpected woman walks onto the stage. This loud and abrupt woman then begins to cluck like a chicken. The dreamer is now mortified because she knows this woman! Initially the crowd laughs at the woman on stage but the dream then takes a turn. The crowd laughs at the woman on stage and the dreamer, too! Moments later she wakes up.

What starts off as an easygoing dream ends up in shame. The dreamer is forced to come face-to-face with the fact that she recognizes herself in the dream figure—that she is inextricably linked to her, so much so that the audience is laughing at them both. She is ashamed, made to feel ridiculous, and mortified in the dream.

In her waking life, the dreamer was often criticized for speaking harshly and out of turn—in fact, many of her relationships ended abruptly because of this. She always believed that the other people were to blame, but in reality she was the person who often ended these relationships, and rather cuttingly so.

She felt that they were callous in in their judgment of her (do you sense a general motif yet?). On the surface it may seem that the other people were in fact judgmental—and they may have been. Yet, her dream tells her that there is something deeper at play, something other than just the external behavior of these people.

The dream figure on stage is a personified aspect of the dreamer's behavior. The woman who clucks like a chicken is a part of herself that she is unwilling to acknowledge.

We know this because the dreamer knows the speaker personally and is ashamed to be associated with her. (The crowd also laughs at *both* of them.) On some level she knows that she is like this woman but she doesn't want to recognize this or to even be connected with her.

So her dream comes to cluck at her—to show her—that whether she accepts it or not, she does in fact behave like the woman on stage. We could say that this woman is inflated and speaking out of turn in order to be center stage and get attention rather than enter into mutual discourse and enjoyment.

So her dream arrives as a rather rude awakening, but a helpful one nonetheless. As a result of her dream wisdom she began to work on cultivating more empathy both for herself and others. She stepped out of the realm of guilt and shame. Rather than looking for confirmation and acceptance from the crowd she began to increase self-validating behaviors. As a result, the quality and degree of intimacy of her relationships improved and she felt more authentically supported by the people in her life.

If you have a dream in which you feel a strong aversion to a dream figure, dig deep and ask yourself whether you are similar to them in any way. We all have blind spots and this is nothing to be ashamed of! These sorts of dream figures come to shine a light on what is hidden in the recesses of the mind yet actively influencing behavior. These hidden, shadowy, and usually uncomfortable figures speak to unconscious motivators and deep-seated beliefs. They present themselves this way so that you will address them and so that "they" no longer have control over you.

That said, frightening or disarming dream figures can also be a reflection or commentary on an external situation that you are willingly participating in, or emotions that are engulfing you. For example:

A client of mine had a dream that she was outside of her house, standing in the street. At first she was looking at her house and not really thinking about anything. Then, as is the way in dreams, she suddenly turned to look up ahead on the road. She noticed a group of darkly cloaked and veiled figures standing threateningly in the distance. At first there were three of them. Then she looked again and noticed they were actually five intimidating figures and that they had begun to move toward her.

Now she's starting to panic, so she starts to look for her keys. (At this point in the dream she is no longer standing outside of her house; she's farther away.) She drops her keys on the ground and as she crouches down to get them, she looks up to see that an entire mob is now encircling her. In that moment they demand that she take them to her house! She wakes up from the sheer terror of the dream.

On reflection, the dream's meaning came to light. In her waking life she felt that she had become absorbed with social media. In actuality, it was more like a borderline addiction that she hadn't really wanted to come to terms with. In her own words she described her pull toward social media thus: "It's like watching a car crash unfurling in slow motion and not being able to do a damn thing. . . ." She often found that as she continued to scroll, her anxiety rose drastically.

In her dream she is standing outside of her house (a place of safety). She is standing in the street (a communal space traversed by many people—the social media app) in front of her house. The house here has a dual symbolic meaning. First, the house represents the state of her psyche. The second symbolic reference can speak to the "house" within the social media app. (There's a home page on most social media apps.) Much like furnishing a house, we can curate the space and entertain "guests." And conversely we are invited to other peoples' homes, too.

She's outside of her place of safety (her house) but close enough to it on the street (at first she feels safe). She's not really doing anything or thinking about anything. She's just standing there. (These are the circumstances that usually prompt her to get onto social media in the first place—boredom and the need to be distracted when she's not really doing anything.)

In the distance stand three darkly cloaked figures who feel threatening to her.

At first it's "not too bad," she says—it's just a few people in the distance. (This situation draws her attention to how she dismisses her instincts in her waking life. She feels threatened and anxious but overrides her body's signals telling her that something is not right.) The dream figures are also veiled and cloaked, which means that they are likely symbolic of people that she doesn't know well in her waking life. Or perhaps aspects of herself that she is unwilling to see (they are "cloaked" from her conscious awareness).

Suddenly, she finds that she is no longer standing outside of her house (she has unexpectedly gone beyond the confines of what is psychologically comfortable). I think almost all of us can empathize with random scrolling and ending up, twenty minutes later, distracted, anxious, and uncomfortable!

She has the cognizance to look for the keys to her house (at this point she wants to return to safety). Keys are formidable dream symbols as they unlock spaces for us. In the word itself the meaning is gifted: key! This is significant—please keenly pay attention!

She finds her keys but drops them. (She finds a way out of the situation, but then loses it). The dream here is showing her that she holds the power to alter her behavior but that her hold on it is tenuous. Her willpower is the key but she needs to work on it. She is unmotivated.

Suddenly, the darkly veiled mob is upon her. She is crouching down to pick up her keys when she sees them. (She's in a vulnerable position but has some power because she has found her keys.) They demand that she take them to her house and let her in.

My client told me that she remembers being horrified in the dream but that they hadn't intended to hurt her physically there and then. That the mob wanted to be in her house *first* was what actually frightened her. In fact, it was that very thought that forced her to wake up from her nightmare! After understanding her dream and the wisdom it conveyed, she took control of her social media viewing for the betterment of her mental health and well-being.

If you too find yourself dreaming of shadowy, dark, veiled, frightening, aggressive figures in your dreams, ask yourself: Am I like this dream figure in any way? Is this figure representative of how I feel? Is this figure speaking to the masculine or feminine aspects of me? Are these dream figures persecuting me in order to show me a situation in my life where the same thing is happening?

Ultimately you ask these questions so that you can choose which action to take in your life for positive personal growth and well-being. Through the discomfort of facing these uncomfortable aspects and emotions we are awakened to find deeper meaning and personal growth within.

Through the use of creativity, you can also work with aspects of dreams that feel unclear or difficult. That is, to allow your creativity to transmute the dream figures (or dream scenes/symbols) into something else as needed or to simply bring them more fully into conscious awareness. This can be done through music, dancing, weaving, clay making, or any art practice that feels right to you. This methodology works for some, but not for all. For those still yearning for a deeper exploration, lucid dreaming is a wonderful path forward for ultimate transformation and personal growth.

Now that you have a firm comprehension of how your emotions, thoughts, and instincts influence your dreams, you are ready to explore lucid dreaming. All that you have learned so far can influence your lucid dreamscapes, so having a greater understanding of your own psyche was a vital step in order for you to actually become a proficient lucid dreamer.

CHAPTER 7

THE LIMINAL SPACE BETWEEN
BEING AWAKE AND ASLEEP

I would like to take you on a journey to the precipice of being awake and asleep. So, for a moment, please close your eyes and simply think about the experience you have as you are about to fall asleep. You know, that drowsy feeling when you're zoning in and out just before you're about to fall into slumber. In that moment you are actually crossing over into the liminal space between wakeful and sleep consciousness. Scientifically speaking, this in-between stage of consciousness is known as the hypnagogic state.

In the hypnagogic state you are neither fully awake nor fully asleep. You are on the precipice between wakefulness and sleep. And with that change, what you perceive begins to change. The word itself etymologically means to "lead into sleep." The hypnagogic shows that we actively experience consciousness on a continuum. *There is a spectrum of consciousness between being awake, being asleep, and dreaming.*

Let's illuminate this spectrum with a metaphor:

Imagine that you are standing in a bedroom in a house. You open the door of this bedroom only to see a long passageway. At the end of this passageway is another door leading into another bedroom. You leave the first room, walk down the passageway, open the door, and walk into the second bedroom.

The first bedroom is your waking life. The passageway is the hypnagogic state. The second bedroom is your dream life.

If you can walk with attention from the first bedroom to the second bedroom, you've journeyed from waking reality to dream reality, but with conscious awareness!

Shamans often do this practice as a form of vision quest, in order to gain lucidity and experience nonlocal consciousness (aka spirit) for assistance. It's also a practice I love to guide participants through in my workshops. You can try this process tonight if you like.

Next time you are in bed but before you are about to fall asleep, begin to pay attention to what arises when you close your eyes. At first you will see darkness but then you may be surprised to notice specks of light, or fragments of shapes, and squiggles that move around.

You may also hear sounds.

These visual images and audible sounds can be alarming to some people—particularly the first time. So it is helpful to remember that they are simply indicators that you are experiencing the hypnagogic state. (If you feel frightened, just move your body, and open your eyes—waking yourself up in the process!)

Don't try to force anything. Simply try to watch what is occurring with a relative level of detachedness and ease. If you can relax into this state while still maintaining awareness, you will begin to notice that these shapes and lights then become images.

These images are usually static at first, as if you're looking at a photograph that is mounted on a wall, but eventually they will turn into three-dimensional scenes—much like the way we experience waking life. The art of this is in maintaining your conscious awareness so that you can move from waking consciousness into dream consciousness lucidly.

I want to stress here that in this case you do not lose consciousness as usual when you simply go to bed and fall asleep. This method feels like you are "walking" yourself into sleep and then (if you can sustain your attention long enough) into dreaming.

The static hypnogogic imagery goes from being flat and lifeless to being animated all around you. Just as the people or furniture in the room are all around you in the room that you are sitting in, as you read this book. Simply take your eyes off this page for a moment and look up to understand what I mean!

That said, the first time I had a hypnagogic experience it really shook my world. Here's my experience:

On closing my eyes, I didn't see anything other than blackness, and I really had to be patient to see the squiggly lines, lights, and shapes generally associated with this state. I usually either fell asleep, unable to remain conscious through the exercise, or I simply kept myself awake while trying too hard to focus on the shapes that accompany the hypnagogic state. It was really frustrating. I tried this exercise for more than a week before I had any success with it.

Then one night I decided to try again, but this time I focused on cultivating a feeling of ease before I attempted this practice. I thought about all the times that life just flowed for me—when things came easily and wonderfully. I thought about experiences that felt good to feel and to remember. This then put me into a quiet and comfortable state of relaxation and ease. I simply relaxed my whole body and mind. Resting in the spaces between my breaths, I was steadily starting to feel more tired, so I tried the practice again.

This time I closed my eyes and the inevitable blackness followed. I relaxed and simply watched the long white shapes form. At first they looked like squiggles, then they became oblong. Loosely I focused on the imagery. I could feel that I just wanted to let myself fall asleep, so I refocused my attention once again, but with a softer awareness than I had tried on the previous attempts. (A good way of knowing if you are practicing soft awareness is to pay attention to your face muscles. Are you squeezing them tightly? If so, you're trying too hard— simply relax.)

Slowly the long white shapes started to change and form into a picture. I was looking at this picture, which looked like something out of a Henri Rousseau exhibition. It was a beautiful image of a jungle featuring monkeys and bright green leaves. I moved to take a closer look at the image of the monkeys. Then all of a sudden I was not looking at the picture. *It was like I was in the picture.* Or more accurately: it was like the picture was now around me with a monkey standing right next to me.

It felt as real as anything else I've experienced.

The surprise that I experienced as a result of that process is an understatement. I was jarred awake and couldn't get back to sleep for a couple of hours after that! (It's very amusing to me that my first hypnagogic image was of monkeys—perhaps a very symbolic and unsubtle representation of my monkey mind!)

At the time, I didn't really understand the ramifications of what this "walking through consciousness" did for some of my permeating belief systems. Despite having experienced many lucid dreams prior to that point!

The reason for that is that before my first hypnagogic experience, I had only ever become lucid in my dreams *after* I had fully fallen asleep.

So, generally my head would hit the pillow and it was lights out for my consciousness! That is, up until something in the dream triggered my awareness to alert me to the fact that I was actually dreaming. Much like the dream example that I shared with you in the opening chapter of this book, where a woman randomly finds herself standing on a street having no recollection of how she got there, only to then become lucid in the dream through self-reflective questioning. *How did I get here? Where was I before this?*

So when I actively "walked" my waking consciousness through the hypnagogic state, fully into dreaming (with active awareness) it seriously rocked my world!

Here's why: We tend to think of our waking and dream lives as completely separate, or at least I did up until that point. You have your waking life where the real stuff happens and then you have your dream life where this other, crazier stuff happens. And again in my lucid dreams, I always fell asleep first and only then became conscious later, which in turn really solidified my belief of separation.

However, remaining conscious through that in-between state of the hypnagogic shattered the belief of separation for me. I guess the illusion that my waking life is where everything happens and defines who I really am ceased to be true for me from that moment. Now that I am much more experienced with the hypnagogic state I understand how pivotal it is as a spiritual practice. If you can become experienced in this practice, you will be able to use your dreams to their full capacity. And with that, you will be able to request greater spiritual guidance and assistance with more ease than with what may be currently available to you. (We'll explore how to do this fully in the upcoming chapters.)

For the most part when you are dreaming regularly (non-lucidly), you are who you believe yourself to be in the dream. The dream self is who you identify with. It's only on waking that you realize you were dreaming. In a dream most of us do not know our waking self. We simply are who we are in the dream.

For example: have you ever dreamed that you were of a different race, gender, or ethnicity? For all intents and purposes you believe that you are that person until you wake up and realize otherwise. This kind of dream practice radically alters beliefs of identity. It also speaks to us about our innate oneness as human beings.

Our waking lives and dream lives are not really separate. Consciousness is not split, but our perception of it is—and our perception is influenced by many things. Such as what we are taught to believe, how we feel, and our experiences.

Think about it in this way: Have you ever considered buying a specific car only to then notice that same type of car everywhere? It's a similar thing. Your perception is like a laser beam that points out where your attention is. That is because you've cognitively primed yourself to notice the same thing over and over again, *regardless of any other information (or cars!) that may be there.*

This rings true with identity too. We get so caught up in labels of identity (race/gender/class/etc.) when really we are so much more than just our physicality and all that comes with it. This also rings true with what we label as reality and dreaming.

Waking consciousness is not all that there is. Dream consciousness is not all that there is. We are held in equanimity between different levels of consciousness through our ability to perceive things through our awareness. An awareness that ultimately has nothing to do with physical sight or the body.

Perspective and the perception of consciousness are wonderful things. They are self-realizing qualities. Beyond your dream self or your waking self, who or what are you? And what would you like to experience as consciousness? The free-writing exercise attached to the end of this chapter will help you to begin to explore this concept more fully.

THE HYPNOPOMPIC STATE

Now, if you can walk your consciousness from waking into dreaming, can you then walk it back from dreaming into waking? The answer is: yes—you can! Using the original metaphor of the two bedrooms connected by a passageway, the hypnopompic state is like the hypnogogic state but in reverse.

So you are in the second bedroom, and you open the door to the passageway. You walk through the passageway and back into the first bedroom. The second bedroom is the place where you dream. The passageway is the hypnopompic state. The first bedroom is your waking life reality.

The hypnopompic state is often overlooked in dream work because most people today seldom have time to luxuriate with their waking-up process. Yet, if you can cultivate awareness of the hypnopompic state you will see an increase in creativity and you'll be able to recall your dreams better—as well as being able to receive helpful and insightful information in a "flash" moment. Just like an "aha" moment! Or what I like to call "aha-insights."

These insights often speak to the dreams you've just experienced and they also can illuminate problems that you've been struggling with. Most of the time they are one-liners and easy to remember. For example:

I had gone to bed stressed as to whether I should give up on a goal that I had been trying to achieve in my waking life. I wanted to achieve my goal but movement was so slow that I hadn't experienced any markers of success prior to that point.

Upon waking I had an aha-insight, which was: "Only a fool gives up so close to the finish line!" I used this insight to summon my courage to push forward and I achieved my goal a few weeks later. Other times, these hypnopompic aha-insights can sound like a disembodied voice (different from your own) that you hear in your mind. For example, one of my clients, Priyanka,* had the following aha-insight on waking: "Don't sign the deal."

At the time, Priyanka was in the process of merging her company with another and everything seemed in place and in order. But then she woke up with this insight and couldn't shake the feeling that she should listen to it. Intellectually it didn't make sense—everything about the deal appeared above board. In fact, it would make her a very wealthy woman. So why this insight?

As a result she decided to simply delay signing the deal. Three weeks later, the company she was potentially going to partner with was implicated in legal proceedings. If she'd merged, her brand would have been tainted and her business would have suffered. Here, her hypnopompic aha-insight really saved her.

These are just two examples of the kinds of aha-insights that you can experience. I've simply learned to listen to these insights acutely. Sometimes they're big and dramatic, as with Priyanka's experience. Other times they're just a commentary of an internal process that you're dealing with. They can also be a summary of the dream experience you've just had—something that is really worth remembering from the dream. It's all helpful!

A FREE-WRITING EXERCISE: DISCOVERING THE "I AM"

Do you believe that you are part of consciousness or do you believe you just experience consciousness? This is a big question that I hope you will honor by spending some time exploring what it means to you. If you can control your actions in your dreams, then who or what is controlling the whole landscape? The following exercise is designed to help you explore your own answers to these big questions.

What You Will Need:

- A pen and notebook.
- A time and place where you won't be disturbed.

When You Are Ready:

- Simply finish this statement: I Am _____.

The idea with free writing is that you just write whatever comes to mind. Don't worry about being grammatically correct or neat. Just write and write. You should keep going until you feel that you've exhausted this statement.

Once I did this exercise and it took me around an hour to complete, and on another occasion it took about ten minutes. The time it takes is irrelevant; what is important is that you really go for it and try to exhaust all possible "I Ams." This is also a great exercise to come back to over and over again if you feel like self-criticism or self-importance has a hold on you!

HERE ARE SOME EXAMPLES

I am consciousness experiencing itself

I am spirit expressing itself

I am a son

I am a man

I am a woman

I am alive

I am a peaceful activist

I am an engineer/mother/friend/lover/wife

I am handing this over to you

Once you are finished with this exercise, go back and scratch out any identifiers of yourself that can change. For example, anything that you can lose or that can change over time (like a job title or hair color). When you do this, two things happen: the first is that you uncover your own beliefs about who you are (for better or worse). The second is that you dive deep into your own beliefs of permanence and imper-manence.

CHAPTER 8

THE DELIBERATE DREAMER

My husband and I were due for a holiday after a series of events had left us feeling rather exhausted. In order to reset we booked a vacation apartment in a small seaside town, looking forward to some real relaxation and rest. It was a picture-perfect location boasting white sand beaches and turquoise sea.

As we arrived the sound of the sea began to soothe away our stress, lifting a layer and then another with each ebb and flow. The beach apartment was perfect for our needs: quiet, comfortable, and close to everything we'd need. We were deeply content and basking in the ease of it all. That is, until our new neighbors moved in.

Justin and Amanda were wonderful people, but they were noisy neighbors, which wasn't what we had envisioned for our Zen vacation. One day, after their third rendition of the same song, we knew we needed to say something.

We eventually mustered up the courage to politely air our concerns to our new neighbors. In response, they seemed surprised, having no idea that they were being that loud. They made a small effort to keep the noise level down and we made an effort to be less bothered by it all, but it didn't get much better than that.

We squeezed in as much joy and sleep as we possibly could out of our vacation, actively practicing acceptance and surrender with every off-key note. Before we knew it our vacation was over, we were back at home and in the full swing of our everyday lives.

One night, deep into sleep, I was dreaming of being at a work conference (fun, I know!) when I heard Justin singing. In my dream, I murmured to myself, "Justin, why must you be so fucking loud?" As it turns out, in my dreams I like to swear like a drunken sailor, deeply emphasizing the uck in fuck, making sure that I am heard. Now, before you potentially analyze my swearing as a marker for repression in my waking life, please let me put your mind at ease. It's more likely that I swear in any and all of the space-time realities in which I exist.

Now back to Justin.

Justin, what the fuck are you doing here and must you be so loud!? My annoyance with Justin had followed me into my dreams. We'd left that vacation. We'd left that apartment rental. *Justin can't be here. I'm back at home. I must be dreaming. This is a dream. I'm dreaming. Stop yelling at Justin.*

Any lucid dream begins the moment that you become fully aware of the fact that you are dreaming when you are in the actual dream. In fact, that is the very definition of a lucid dream. I knew that I was dreaming once I recognized that Justin couldn't possibly be at my work conference. I then went on to explore my dream with a level of conscious awareness that was highly unanticipated, actively trying to remain as lucid in my dream, for as long as possible.

After that experience, a voice hilariously identifying as Justin often broadcasts itself to me in my regular dreams, much like an announcement at the airport: "Hey, Athena. It's Justin again. How's it going?" Or I'll dream of turning into a new street aptly named Justin, or a dream figure will mention the name. All of which trigger lucidity.

I enjoy the term "deliberate dreamer" because it encompasses so much of what we experience ourselves to be. We are the deliberate dreamers of both our waking and sleep lives. You are a deliberate dreamer!

My "Justin experiences" and my work with other dreamers has led me to believe that there is a part in all of us that very much wants us to become lucid. Just think about how many times you dream of things that seem weird or out of place. Perhaps all of these things are markers or dream signs clamoring for your awareness so that you can "wake up." *They are your own versions of Justin.*

As you read further on, you will see that I've described many different processes and techniques that you can practice in order to become awake in your dreams. Anyone can lucid dream—that includes you! Dedication and perseverance are required when you are just starting out. Pick a few techniques and try them out consistently until you have your first lucid dream or more frequent lucid dreams.

AN INCREASE IN SELF-REFLECTIVE THINKING CAN TRIGGER LUCID DREAMS

Critical and self-reflective thinking have helped trigger many of the lucid dreams that I've had. In the dream I just described to you, I asked myself: Why is Justin at my work function? My brain was trying to make rational sense of the dream scene it found itself in. It was only when I realized that he couldn't possibly be there that I understood I was dreaming. Self-reflective questioning was the trigger for my lucidity.

This dream is also a good example of a well-known lucid dreaming method called DILD, or dream induced lucid dreaming.

It has been my experience, and that of many of my clients, that the more self-aware and mindful you become in your waking life, the easier it becomes to use the same skill set in your dreams. If you are aware enough to question your reality within a dream, then as a result you will become lucid. Meditation is just one activity that can help cultivate this awareness.

In meditation you begin to become the observer in order to simply witness what arises in the mind. The more that you practice observing your own stream of consciousness, the less at the mercy of it you become. Regular meditation ultimately cultivates a greater and more expansive space between stimulus and response. This liminal space is where self-reflective thinking is heightened. This is the space you actively want to cultivate so that you can trigger yourself awake in your dreams.

Here's a practical and everyday example: Instead of reacting to your mean coworker because she's criticized you again, you simply enter the liminal space between trigger and response. You take no action other than to witness what is arising in you.

Perhaps you begin by simply witnessing your reactive thoughts: "What is her problem? Who does she think she is? Why do people always walk all over me?" Then you move on to witnessing your feelings and your bodily reaction: "I feel so enraged and sick to my stomach." And then, when you feel you have cultivated that inner space enough, you actively choose your response: "Fighting with her won't help me. I'm going to choose to lovingly assert my boundaries. How she behaves has nothing to do with how I choose to respond. I'm going to simply step away."

Much like the previous example, everyday scenarios then become the perfect opportunities to practice self-awareness and empowerment. This is a type of wakeful meditation practice that you can do at any time. You simply begin by focusing all of your attention on the present scenario, or moment, that you find yourself in.

Bringing your full attention to what you are experiencing, you begin to ask yourself self-reflective questions aimed at raising your awareness: What do I see? What sounds do I hear? What scents do I smell? How does my body feel?

Then you move on to simply observing and witnessing the stream of thoughts that are going on within your mind: What am I thinking? All the while noticing any knee-jerk reactions that you may be experiencing in relation to your thoughts and what you are experiencing externally: How am I responding to this situation?

The purpose of these self-reflective questions is to help you gain objective distance and to heighten your ability to consciously respond to whatever is present in your current reality. To develop and activate that liminal space between stimulus and response so that you have greater choice in *how you respond*.

One of benefits of this practice is that you become aware of how you are regularly thinking and feeling, and how you behave as a consequence. Ultimately, this offers you the opportunity to change anything that is no longer working for you, so that you can feel better and live better. This is one of the most liberating practices that anyone can undertake on their journey of personal growth.

It is also a practice that is equally liberating in terms of dream work. That is because it raises your awareness, which means that you can more easily begin to identify things that seem out of place in your dreamscape, triggering lucidity. Like when you see a monkey in your office and then through self-reflection realize that never mind the monkey—you don't even work in an office! So you must be dreaming. Or when you dream of someone who has passed away and you become cognizant of that remembrance. Self-awareness isn't just part of the course of becoming a lucid dreamer (and a conscious co-creator in your waking life), it is a necessity and a goal.

Interestingly enough, the Max Planck Institute of Psychiatry in Germany has done research on discovering which parts of the brain are activated during lucid dreaming versus normal dreaming. They did this by comparing the brain activity of the research participants during both normal and lucid dreaming. The team of scientists at the institute were able to mark the key areas in the brain, which were activated during lucid dreaming using magnetic resonance tomography (MRT).

Their results showed increased activity in a particular cortical network and the respective brain regions (such as the prefrontal cortex and the precuneus) when lucid consciousness was achieved in dreaming. According to these neuroscientists, these are the areas within the brain that are associated with self-assessment, the ability to evaluate one's own thoughts and feelings, and self-perception (that is, metacognition via self-reflectivity).

Their research is groundbreaking because it shows the neural networks of a conscious dream state for the first time. And it confirms that self-reflectivity is linked to lucid dreaming.

THERE ARE MANY PATHWAYS TO LUCID DREAMING

As you expand your self-reflective abilities through cultivating the space between stimulus and response, you may also want to practice multiple methods so that you can increase your odds of experiencing lucid dreaming. I've chosen to list multiple techniques here for your convenience. These methods are based on academic research, creative wisdom, and, equally, what has simply worked well for me and the broader lucid dreaming community.

REALITY CHECK #1: AM I IN A DREAM?

Throughout the course of your day you want to deliberately "reality test" your waking life. That means you are going to ask yourself whether you are in a dream. Ask yourself this question multiple times during the course of your day. For example, you can ask yourself this question every time you eat or every hour on the hour. You literally say: Is this a dream? The idea is that when you are then in an actual dream the same question should instinctively pop up in your mind. Your answer will be: Yes! I am in a dream.

I have had many clients who have found this method highly successful. Yet, at one stage in my life, when I was trying to rekindle my ability to lucid dream, I practiced this for about three months without any success. I'm not saying this to dishearten you; my point is simply that becoming a lucid dreamer is really an experiential process. And you may well have to try many different methods, multiple times, until one of them works for you. So please don't give up if it takes you slightly longer than you were anticipating! Simply practice and enjoy the process.

REALITY CHECK #2: ARE YOU EXPERIENCING LIFE IN FIRST OR THIRD PERSON?

This method really helped me to experience many more lucid dreams. Have you ever had a dream where it felt like you were watching a movie? In essence it's like you are experiencing your dream in third person. In other words, you observe yourself interacting with other people in your dream from an aerial (or distant) view and because of that you realize that you are dreaming.

We don't see ourselves in our entirety in our everyday lives unless we watch a video recording of ourselves or see our reflection in the mirror. So if you begin to frequently pay attention to how you perceive the world, you may then be able to carry that mindfulness through into your dream consciousness, which can then trigger lucidity. Throughout the course of the day you can ask yourself: Am I experiencing life in first person?

Please note that although this method and many of the other ones are targeted for individuals who have sighted capacities, it speaks to something larger than just seeing, that is, the ability to question how you perceive and assimilate the perceptual information you are receiving all day (and then night!) long. We experience life through our senses, and getting in tune with all of them can help to heighten self-awareness, which in turn can assist in lucidity.

Research also indicates that blind people can have visually-based dreams in some cases. That said, the ability to do so is often influenced by whether the dreamer lost their sight after the age of seven or before, or if they were born blind. Yet to date, as far as I am aware, there haven't been any scientific studies done to prove whether blind people can in fact experience lucid dreams. My gut instinct is to say that lucid dreaming is about how we experience consciousness, not sight, so being able to see should not necessarily be a prerequisite. Perhaps one of you, dear readers, knows someone like this?

REALITY CHECK #3: DO YOU LOOK LIKE YOU?

Here is another reality check that you can practice during the course of your waking life. Every time you see your reflection in a mirror, pay attention to what you actually look like. Practice a few focused moments of just observing yourself. My clients have found this reality check most effective when they are able to silence, or move past, any judgmental thoughts that pop up. If you are highly critical of what you look like, you may want to focus instead on one of the other reality checks.

Oftentimes in our dreams, we will see ourselves but we don't actually look the same. You may look like you but with altered elements, such as having a different hair color or being taller. Alternatively, you may look completely different in a dream. You may be a six-foot-tall man with striking features when in reality you are a petite woman. The goal with all of these reality checks is to trigger your self-reflective awareness.

REALITY CHECK #4: LOOK AT YOUR HANDS

Look at your hands intermittently throughout the course of your day. Really look at them and pay attention to them. In your dreams your hands may very well look different. If you can recognize any difference, that recognition can then trigger lucidity. You can also take this reality check one step further by pushing your fingers against the palm of your opposite hand or a table. In a dream, your fingers may very well be able to move through the object you are pushing against.

SPARROW'S WAKE UP, BACK TO BED METHOD

This is one of the simplest and most effective methods that you can do if you don't mind interrupting your sleep. What is great about this method is that it is really easy! Simply wake up a few hours earlier than usual. Then actively stay awake for an hour. Once that hour has passed, go back to sleep. Many of my clients who have practiced this method will set an alarm for 5:30 a.m. This usually gives them enough time to experience a lucid dream before they have to get ready and head out for the day.

DR. STEPHEN LABERGE'S MILD METHOD

MILD stands for the mnemonic initiated lucid dream. This method uses memory, intention, and visualization to help you achieve lucid dreaming. I'm going to outline the four steps involved in this method so that you can experiment with multiple methods.

The first step is being able to recall your dreams. If you can't recall your dreams it's unlikely that you will then be able to remember if you've had a lucid dream. So the idea is to practice dream recall, as much as possible, in order to make it a habit.

If you need a quick refresher, simply lie still on waking and replay your dream in your mind. When you do this you are helping your mind store your dream into memory. Remember to write your dreams down too. Once you are able to easily dream recall, move on to the next step.

The second step is to deliberately practice reality checks throughout the course of your day, such as asking yourself: Is this a dream? Simply practice reality checks as often as you can.

The third step is practiced when you are in bed and preparing to go to sleep. During this time you simply recite affirmations to yourself. For example, you can say, "I am a deliberate and conscious lucid dreamer" or "Tonight I am going to experience a lucid dream." I like to use the following affirmations: "It's really easy for me to lucid dream" and "Lucid dreaming comes naturally and easily to me." A core element of these affirmations is that you say them like you believe them. You state them with wholehearted determination and belief.

The fourth step is to visualize a dream that you can remember. It is important during this final step that you allow yourself to become deeply relaxed. Once you feel very relaxed, begin to visualize a recent and pleasant remembered dream scene. Visualize your dream scene as vividly as you can.

Once you visualize your dream and have played it out for a while, go on to recognize a sign that you are in a dream. Actively visualize a dream sign, or reality check, that signals to you that you are in a dream. Perhaps you notice a strange person, place, or object. And as you notice this dream anomaly, say to yourself, "This is a dream!" You are purposefully visualizing yourself becoming lucid in a dream.

Remember, all of this is happening *before* you've actually fallen asleep. The idea is to vividly create a lucid dream fantasy that is based on a real dream that you've previously experienced. It's like a dress rehearsal for the real thing.

Then in your visualization imagine that you've just become lucid. What would you like to do? Perhaps you picture yourself flying or simply altering other key aspects of your dream. It is all entirely up to you.

You will likely fall asleep during this process, and that is perfectly fine. The core intention behind the MILD technique is simply that the last thought on your mind, before you fall asleep, is that of having a lucid dream. Usually what then happens is that you go on to have an actual lucid dream later on that night.

But if that doesn't happen for you, simply practice and practice until it does.

EXPERIMENTING WITH DREAM STATES DURING A MOMENTARY AFTERNOON NAP

Salvador Dalí, the surrealist artist, whimsically wrote about the creative benefits of wakeful sleep in his book *50 Secrets of Magic Craftsmanship*. In fact, he attributed a lot of his artistic imagery to the things he saw in the hypnogogic and hypnopompic states. So much so that he wrote his book almost as a "how-to" manual for any artist who wants to use sleeping and dreaming as methods to transmute creative art.

Now I know that many people don't have the luxury of taking an afternoon nap daily. But if you can carve out time to practice the following paraphrased exercise, which Dalí called "Slumber with a Key," I think you may be sweetly surprised. Especially if you want to explore and heighten your own creativity!

According to Dalí, here's what you'll need: a bony leather chair (ideally of Spanish craftsmanship), a heavy key, and a plate. Here's what you'll need to do:

Place the plate, upside down, on the floor. Then lean back into the bony leather chair. Fear not if you do not have an uncomfortable chair of Spanish make! Simply use what you have. Then delicately place the heavy key on your left hand, specifically resting it on both your forefinger and thumb. Now here's the essential ingredient to this practice: you don't want to fall asleep for more than a few minutes. Dalí maintained that anything over a minute may even be too long!

That is why the key is so precariously placed on your hand: shortly after you have fallen asleep you are woken up by the key unceremoniously falling from your hand, banging loudly against the upside-down plate. According to Dalí, a minute or two of slumber is all that your inner processes need to give you the instinctive information with which you should create.

On recalling these hypnopompic images you should then immediately create, unencumbered by any logical thoughts that you may have, most importantly, how you think a piece of creative work should turn out. Simply create using what you have experienced during your sleep as your medium.

I love Dalí's method for a few reasons. The first is that it is great to carve out a specific time when you can focus on your creativity and dreams. It signifies to you and those around you that you honor your inner world. In psychological terms we would say that it affords you the opportunity to intentionally explore your intrapsychic processes. Consequentially, through every afternoon slumber you will strengthen both your instinctual life and spiritual life.

I also love this method because it is so jarring in its design that it's hard not to remember your dream imagery when you are so rudely awakened! This in itself helps to increase dream recall. And if you can fall asleep in a bony chair you are self-promoted to the status of "expert sleeper," able to conquer all forms of cheap air travel. Lastly and perhaps most importantly it increases creativity and play in a far too serious world.

STABILIZING YOUR LUCID DREAMS THROUGH EMOTIONAL MINDFULNESS

So, you've just become lucid in a dream for the first time ever—what a wonderful moment of awakening! So much so that the sheer excitement knocks you right out of your slumber. I have woken myself up from more lucid dreams than I care to admit, simply because I've gotten too excited about the realization that I was, in fact, dreaming. This is a common experience when you are starting out on your journey of becoming a frequent lucid dreamer and nothing to get disheartened about.

Part of the practice of becoming a deliberate dreamer is being able to quickly emotionally regulate in your dreams. In order to stay lucid, so that you can benefit from the maximum time within your dreams, you need to be able to stay calm and ground your emotional state, whatever it may be. An effective way to practice emotional regulation is by becoming more mindful in your waking life on a day-to-day (if not a moment-to-moment) basis.

If you can become emotionally proficient in your waking life, you can carry that skill through to your dream life, ultimately calming your emotions once you become aware of the fact that you've just become conscious in your dream. The more often you can observe (or witness) your own emotions and thoughts in your waking life, the easier it is to become less reactively influenced by them and to alter them as necessary in your dream life.

A MINDFULNESS PRACTICE:
FOCUS ON YOUR FEET

A great mindfulness practice that you can focus on to stay calm in your lucid dream is to fully bring your attention to your feet. I recommend that you do this practice in both your waking and dream life. Try and practice this exercise sporadically throughout your day and specifically when you feel like an external situation is starting to get the better of you.

In essence, the practice is simple: deliberately bring your attention to your feet at random times during the course of your day. Notice the physical sensations of your feet against the ground or in your shoes. How do your toes feel? Are they hot or cold? Do you feel comfortable? Are your feet stiff? Move them around, noticing any new physical sensations that you feel. Do this practice for as long as necessary. The idea is to wholly bring your attention to your feet to streamline your awareness and control your focus.

In doing so, because you've taken mindful control over what you are placing your attention on, you also stop any automatic thoughts that you may be thinking and any emotions that you may be experiencing. I do this practice at least twelve times a day, when I'm in a queue, stuck in traffic, preparing food, watching TV, drinking coffee, and really just going about my routine. I've found that it has helped me to reclaim my ability to focus my thoughts and emotions in the present moment.

Equally, when I become lucid in a dream I quickly try to focus on my feet to interrupt the excitement that I feel. Because I've made it a habitual practice in my waking life, I've found that it has become easier to implement in my dreams, too. So if you've just become lucid in a dream, and you get excited, try to then quickly focus on your feet to interrupt any exhilaration that you may be experiencing so that you don't wake up!

There's also another great reason for this exercise, which is that when you pay attention to your body in a dream you begin to ground the dream itself while you focus your attention at the same time. Some lucid dreamers take this one step further by shouting "dream stabilize" at the dreamscape in order to stabilize the dream! This has worked well for many people, including myself, and so you should give it a go if you are a beginner lucid dreamer.

CHAPTER 9

I'M LUCID—NOW WHAT?

The details are fuzzy but the feeling is clear: I'm nervous. I'm tense because I am free-falling from the sky. I am hurtling down at an alarming rate. As I continue to fall I see a range of clouds in front of me. I descend through them. An uncomfortable realization then comes to mind: these clouds are cold to the touch.

Now I'm feeling intensely cold, and I hate feeling cold, and I become acutely aware of how much it will actually hurt when I hit the ground. Still splashes of pale blue sky and white clouds graphically grip my vision despite my resistance. I move my head to the side while closing my eyes in order to stop seeing these fast-moving images. Free-falling is making me nauseated.

Then a life-saving thought dominates my sensory overload: *When exactly did I jump out of a plane?* Then a follow-on thought: *How can this be happening?* Boom! Lightbulb moment: I now know that I am dreaming. In a few split seconds, I go from the free-falling suspense and dreaded expectation of hitting the ground, to actively and deliberately flying in my lucid dream.

I fly through the clouds and it amuses me that they still make me feel cold even though I am now deliberately dreaming and it feels incredible! Sensations in lucid dreams are very tactile. You will come to experience this firsthand the more you lucid dream.

I stop flying and decide to land in the unknown dreamscape below me. In this lucid dream the thought of landing is enough to "materialize" me there. In the distance I see my brother. In our waking lives we live in different countries, so to say that I am happy to see him is an understatement. I wave to grab his attention and through my enthusiasm, I unintentionally wake myself up!

As you come to explore your lucid dreams more, you will see that deliberate dreaming is heavily influenced by remaining emotionally mindful throughout the course of the dream, or for as long as possible. That said, your lucid dreams are as limitless as your intentions, so what do you want to experience in your lucid dreams?

Want to fly? Will it so. Want to experience breathing underwater? Done. Ready to explore the past? Go ahead. Want to discover what the next right action is? Ask the dreamscape. Once you're done with all the "fun stuff" you can even dig deep and discover why you are here and what your soul purpose is! Or request to meet your own guide. The possibilities are endless.

Beginner lucid dreamers often ask me if lucid dreaming is like experiencing virtual reality. And my answer is always no. With virtual reality you see things in a very lifelike way but you can't feel them. For example, in a virtual reality experience you can explore Italy but you won't be able to taste the gelato! (How disappointing, in my opinion—like, what's the point?) But in a lucid dream you can will yourself to Italy where you can eat the gelato and it will feel real, tactile, and no-doubt delicious!

Lucid dreaming is like waking reality but with a different set of natural laws that govern your experience. It feels as real as life but you can materialize and interact with the dream world simply by will of thought. You can heal by moving your hand over your body simply with the intent to heal. You can fly. You can breathe underwater. In fact, breathing underwater means you've just become more proficient in lucid dreaming because your physical body isn't there—it's your ethereal or energetic essence. And does that really need to breathe?

In any case, the more lucid dreams you have, the more you will see that you don't need to abide by the same physical rules that apply in waking life. For example, in a lucid dream you don't necessarily need to open a door that appears in the dream, you can simply walk straight through it! (Much like ghosts do in popular movies! Ha!) You aren't limited by physicality but you still feel. It is wonderful paradox that can feel hard to accept until you experience it for yourself.

The larger philosophical framework that you believe in will also influence how you behave in your lucid dream experiences. It's also helpful to remember that the initial dreamscape itself springs forth without your consciously doing anything. For example, it's generally when you already find yourself in a dream that you become lucid and then interact with what you see. So ultimately you have some control but not omnipotent control. You are still experiencing the dream world, even though you can manipulate or influence aspects of it. Moreover, as you come to explore the chapter on lucid dream figures you will see that the dream world is unlikely to be a conceptual place designed solely by the mind—but more on that later!

All in all, lucid dreaming is wonderful. You will also find that your emotions, memories, and psyche can and will influence what you experience in your lucid dreams. That is why I spent a good portion of this book walking you through the unconscious, the influence of emotions, and the symbolic nature of dreaming. You need to have a handle on all three of these topics because your awareness of them can greatly influence your lucid dream experiences. You will also see that the symbolic nature of dreaming can carry through to lucid dreaming, so it's helpful to understand symbols (which you now have a much better grasp on through simply reading the earlier chapters of this book).

Now, let's explore some of the most common areas that people like to initially focus on in their lucid dreams: physical healing, emotional betterment, dream travel, shape-shifting, and receiving spiritual guidance. Remember, your lucid dreaming experience is unique to you, so you can choose what to focus on.

THE BASICS

If you've never had a lucid dream, then there are few things that are very helpful to know up front. First, when you find yourself lucid in the dreamscape you will notice that the imagery, place, or people that triggered your lucidity remain there. So you've just woken up (so to speak) to the fact that you are dreaming. What surrounds you? At that point you can choose to explore that dream reality, as I did with the flying dream experience that I shared with you at the beginning of this chapter. I just went with the flow and experienced the dream as it unfolded.

Or you can wipe the slate clean and dream with a deliberate intention.

For example, if you are trying to lucid dream in order to heal a problem that you can't resolve in your waking life, flying is of no help to you! It's helpful to first stabilize the dream as quickly as possible so that you remain lucid longer. So you stabilize the dream to ground yourself into the process—again, you can do this by bringing your attention to your feet and calming your dream body. You can also do this by simply saying the words "dream stabilize" or through rubbing your hands together. Words are incredibly powerful in lucid dreams, so use yours mindfully!

Then you can clear out any psychological projections that are active in the dreamscape. Author and lucid dreamer Robert Waggoner has a wonderful practice where he simply recommends saying: "All thought-forms begone!" This practice aims to remove the psychological projections of the mind so that one can work with more luminous aspects of self and spirit. In essence, everything that remains in the dreamscape is then no longer just a projection from your own mind but rather spirit. (We'll explore this concept more fully in the chapter on lucid dream figures; for now, just trust in the process of application.)

Once you've cleared out the projections of thought from the lucid dream, declare your intention to the dreamscape. You can think it or say it out loud. Do this as often as required or up until something changes in the dreamscape. I like to say, "As the energy that created this dream please help me to—" and then I express my intention.

If you need to wake up from your lucid dream because you are feeling afraid, frightened, or simply overwhelmed (it happens to all of us!), simply *will yourself awake.* You can say "wake up" or you can focus on opening your eyes. I've had lucid dreams in which I've experienced intense vibrations and sounds that often make me feel nervous (although I shouldn't be) so I wake myself up. With practice you will become more and more comfortable with your lucid dream experiences!

Most of us avid lucid dreamers have the issue of wanting to remain lucid for longer, not wanting to get out of the dream faster. That said, *you have power in a dream*, so use it as you need it. Remember, you can materialize anything that you need simply by willing it so!

HEALING IN YOUR LUCID DREAMS

Could you heal yourself in a lucid dream and see a physical change in your body or a lessening of symptoms the following morning? From my own experiences, and that of my workshop participants, I know that you can alter physical symptoms if your intention is crystal clear and you are willing to persevere! From authors Robert Waggoner's and Ed Kellogg's seminal lucid dream research, the answer to whether you can heal in a dream and see physical changes the next morning is both yes and no. It all depends on the dreamer.

Their published research showed that some lucid dreamers did experience a lessening of painful symptoms, or a quickening of the healing experience, or even a total absence of the problem on waking after they actively worked on healing in their lucid dreams. Sadly, for other lucid dreamers their healing attempts were totally unsuccessful.

Waggoner found that the people who generally had successful lucid dreams in which they healed an ailment (or who found a general improvement on waking) hit five core features in their lucid dreams: they had active belief, expectation, focus, intent, and will all aimed toward healing.

They were, for lack of a better term, *in it to win it*!

Successful lucid dreamers often dreamed of a doctor, or an Inner Healer, a Guardian that would help them to heal right then and there. Or they would picture a symbolically healing place like a fountain or the sea, and get into the water. One dreamer even called forth a glass and then filled it with healing "medicine," actively drinking the elixir in their dream—only to wake up feeling much better.

What's important to note here is that all the successful dreamers healed in the dream. They believed they could and so they did. They also weren't given something to take back and do in waking life (although this can happen, as you will see in a later dream example).

Some people argue that this is the placebo effect. My response is that even if that is so (I don't believe it is!), waking up without a physical ailment is so much better than feeling sick. I also believe that the effects of belief in a lucid dream are more powerful because the energy body is being worked with, not the physical body per se.

Waggoner's research and my own dream work also reminds me of the importance of persistence. There are no limits on how many times you can try to heal something for the better, in both your dreams and your waking life. Approach your lucid dreams with motivation and curiosity and see where they lead you. There are many pathways to well-being, and lucid dreaming can offer you more than just one way to get there.

Most shamanic practices also focus on this aspect of lucid dreaming: the ability to directly and consciously influence the physical realm through dreams. In metaphysical lingo we would explain this phenomenon as follows: you heal because you merge with source energy with the intention to heal. You remember that the physical world is dreamlike in the sense that it can be altered through—you guessed it—your intention and spiritual essence. Ultimately, nothing is stuck, everything can be transmuted!

Here's another tangible example that shows that you can use your dream time for a waking-life goal. Say that you play the violin or guitar and want to become better at it. You can use your lucid dream to practice becoming more proficient. And it will work!

Research published in the *Journal of Sports Sciences* as well as studies done through Harvard have proven this to be true. For example, practicing specific motor skills (like walking, running, or jumping) in a lucid dream have been scientifically proven to lead to positive improvements in those skills in waking life. And not just that, but as much as is gained practicing the action in waking life. So you can hone a skill in your lucid dreams and see real improvements in your waking life. Can you just imagine the implications of what this means?

Sometimes people worry that being this active in a lucid dream will leave them feeling super tired on waking. This is not usually the case. Most people do not wake up feeling depleted from their lucid dreams. They feel replenished and rested. Of course, this is not always the case for everyone, but it shouldn't be a barrier to lucid dreaming. You'll come to know what works best for you.

The main point here is that there is an active and powerful bidirectional relationship between waking reality and dream reality. Lucid dreaming acts as the bridge between these two realities and your deliberate intention makes all the difference. Do you see why I call you a deliberate and powerful dreamer?

What are you hoping to create or alter in your waking life? What do you need help with? How willing are you to actively interact with the more numinous aspects of existence? What do you need? Use your intention deliberately in your lucid dreams to assist you with any and all of those questions.

Here's another great dream experience that illustrates my point:

A woman was experiencing severe psoriasis. She'd had the issue for over ten years and after countless medical tests nothing ever seemed to resolve the problem. She just learned to live with the persistent skin issue, that is, until she became a lucid dreamer. One night in a dream she "awoke" to the fact that she was dreaming. In her lucid dream she then asked for a guide to appear who could help her to heal her problem.

In a split second (things move very fast in lucid dreams) a man was standing in front of her. He didn't say anything to her but handed her a tiny pillow, so small that it fit into the palm of her hand. As she looked down at the miniature pillow it dissolved into the palm of her hand. But before it did she noticed that the bottom of the pillow was shaped quite strangely.

She memorized the appearance of the dream pillow just before she spontaneously woke up. On waking up she got out of bed and drew the little pillow. Her psoriasis hadn't disappeared through the lucid dream—when she woke up, the issue was still there—but now she had helpful information. Her guide had given her this miniature pillow; but what did it mean?

On reflection she came to realize just how symbolic the pillow was. She needed to take a pill-*ow* in order to feel better. Now, for someone who spent years trying to medically heal the issue this wasn't revelatory news to her. What pill? Pills hadn't helped her thus far. Then she remembered that the pillow was shaped quite strangely. After some research she came to see that the shape of the pillow looked close to what the core chemical structure of penicillin looks like. She then found a doctor who helped her, and after a month of focused treatment her psoriasis disappeared, never to return.

In this example the relationship between the dream world and waking life is so clearly shown.

You can alter physical ailments in a lucid dream or you can use dream information to help you in your waking life. Persist until you've exhausted all possibilities!

LIBERATING EMOTIONS THROUGH
LUCID DREAMING

One of the most beneficial aspects of lucid dreaming is that you can work through your emotions and actively solve problems. Here's a simple exercise to guide you in this process: the next time you are in a lucid dream, call forth the image of the problem, or emotion, that you are struggling with. Then ask the dreamscape for guidance on how to work through the issue.

A dream workshop participant of mine shared a problem that she was hoping to resolve through lucid dreaming. Years ago she had a terrible fight with her sister that left both of them unwilling to speak to the other. Each of them held fast to her position of being "right." Family functions were canceled as neither of them were willing to concede. Their fight created a huge rift within the entire family. The emotional rage and anger that Shelly* felt as a result was palpable, and eventually her anger morphed into bitterness and feelings of loss for what was once a great sisterly relationship. She began to experience deep emotional pain from the fracture of her relationship but was un-willing to admit it. So she decided to dream on it.

In her lucid dream, she stabilized the dream, cleared out projections, and then requested assistance with this problem. In that moment a white ball of light/energy showed up in front of her. Not knowing what to do she said, "Please help me." The ball hovered in and all around her, then moved into what she described as her chest (then abdomen) although she couldn't really see her body. On waking she felt like the emotional heaviness had left her. So much so that she phoned her sister and extended an olive branch, which her sister accepted.

Regarding a more emotionally extreme level, there is also a current body of research aimed at discovering whether PTSD (post-traumatic stress disorder) can be altered via lucid dreaming. Specifically, the frightening nightmares associated with PTSD. The research is incredibly promising, showing that individuals who suffer from PTSD and who learn how to become lucid in their dreams can experience a positive shift toward emotional well-being and betterment. This is usually through confronting the nightmare and altering the landscape/imagery within the lucid dream. Most wonderfully, these nightmares seem to naturally dissipate from that point on.

Regardless of PTSD, in most nightmares we are faced with distressing shadow figures. By shadow figures I simply mean dream people, images, or situations that frighten you. We can face these shadow figures in our lucid dreams in order to experience greater well-being and personal growth. They generally represent the unconscious beliefs you hold or repressed memories and difficult emotions that you are struggling to deal with.

You can work with any of the shadow figures of your psyche by confronting them and embracing them with love and kindness (don't get into a battle with them). You simply turn to face them when you are in the lucid dream. The main thing is to love them and to talk to them if you can.

A note here: facing shadow figures can feel scary.

In traditional Bön Buddhist lucid dreaming practices, before lucid dreamers can even attempt to face certain dream figures they first have to learn to master core elements of the dreamscape, for example, through touching fire. This is to show the dreamer that absolutely nothing in the dreamscape can hurt the dreamer. This is a helpful sentiment to keep in mind—nothing in your dream can hurt you but some experiences require a level of personal skill.

You should be proficient as a lucid dreamer before attempting to work with your shadow figures, or difficult emotions and impulses. Luckily, as I've illustrated earlier in this book, there are many ways to work with our shadow impulses or figures that involve your regular dreams and waking life. For instance, through art journaling, talk therapy, and regular dream work.

When you find that you can alter things in a lucid dream with ease and proficiency, on a regular basis, then it is likely that you are ready to work with your shadow figures via your lucid dreams. Here's an experience of my own shadow integration within a lucid dream:

I was on a pathway of sorts descending a very weird-looking set of steps. It was only when I realized that the steps were made of bone that I actually became lucid in the dream. All of a sudden, random disembodied arms began to grab at my ankles. They really frightened me, and so in response I frantically tried to shake them off me. Finally I said, "I know I'm dreaming. I know that you can't really hurt me!"

Then the "arms" disappeared and I felt deeply relieved.

My relief was short-lived as two very menacing figures then appeared in front of me. They began to laugh (and growl!) at me. I said the same thing once again: "I know I'm dreaming. I know you can't really hurt me!" At this point, I was actually petrified in my lucid dream. Remember, it feels real, so it takes courage to do this kind of dream work.

Centering myself, I watched them move toward me while they morphed into one large, dominating figure. At this point this large figure began to shout at me incoherently. I let it come toward me. Then with my arms wide open, I said, "I know that you are hurt and I love you." In that moment the figure changed into a smaller being that I picked up and held close to my chest. I was unable to maintain lucidity after that and woke up feeling strangely comforted and reassured.

Remember that you always have the strength to wake up if need be or to change the entire dream scene into something totally different in any lucid dream. (All you have to do is say, WAKE UP! in the dream.) So if things are getting a bit too intense, use your power. Remember that the goal in dealing with your shadow figures is to offer them love and compassion. In fact, you may find that you wake up crying or with a great sense of relief as many dreamers do.

You can also ask the dreamscape (in fact, I advise this) to speak to you about issues that you struggle with. Simply ask the dreamscape to show you on a screen what you need to see. This usually requires a high level of focus and attention, so the goal is to remain lucid for as long as possible.

Much like the psyche, there are different levels to lucid dreaming and your intention can and will alter the lucid dream. When you focus your intention (and attention) you will see that you receive active and positive results both in your lucid dreams and your waking life. When we work toward greater personal growth and well-being, we are in essence working with an intrinsically whole system. This is the psyche and our spiritual essence. We do not need to obliterate, remove, or even transcend the system; we simply need to learn how to trust ourselves and use our dreams well.

TRAVELING TO SPECIFIC DESTINATIONS IN YOUR LUCID DREAMS

Now that you've discovered some of the more helpful practical applications of what you can do in a lucid dream, let's explore traveling in the dreamscape. In chapter two I showed you how you can incubate a regular dream. The process to incubate a lucid dream is slightly longer than with regular dreaming unless you already are an experienced lucid dreamer. If you are, then you likely know how to travel to different places simply through using your intention and will well enough in the dream. Lucky you!

However, if you are still new to this practice, it can be helpful to set the intention for your lucid dreams during your day. It's important to really prime your mind and consciousness for the experience you want to have in the dream. The repetition of your intention will increase the likelihood of your having a specific lucid dream. You can use this incubation practice for any type of lucid dream experience that you wish to have, not just for the desire to travel to amazing places in your lucid dreams.

You begin by simply setting your intention during the day. Again the focus here should be on the words you choose to use. It's advisable to actually write down your intention a few times during the course of your day. You can write (or say): "I will lucid dream tonight. When I become aware that I am dreaming I will travel to—" and name whatever place you want to try to experience.

For example, if you want to have a lucid dream in which you see Egypt and the pyramids, you will need to set the intention to do so. The intention could be: "I will lucid dream tonight. When I recognize that I am dreaming I will visit the pyramids in Egypt." Be very clear with your words because the way you word things, or intend things, can influence your lucid dream.

For example, if you worded your intention thus: "I see the pyramids in Egypt," you may have a lucid dream in which you pick up a travel brochure with images of the pyramids on the front cover! In essence, you've incubated your lucid dream, but not exactly for the result you were hoping for. So once again, the words you choose matter; be as specific and concise as possible. (I've incubated many lucid dreams with a slightly ambiguous intention and so have many other lucid dreamers worldwide! Remember, the lucid dream process is experiential and so it does require a level of openness and understanding. The beauty of this is that once you experience success incubating your dreams you can do it over and over again as you see fit.)

Then, once you have found your accurately worded intention with the goal of dream travel, remind yourself that you will become lucid in the dream.

When you are finally ready to go to bed begin to practice systematic relaxation—calm your body and mind. Then, visualize the dream scene you want to experience while repeating your intentions. Using the Egypt example, visualize yourself standing in front of the pyramids. Take in all the desert sand around you. Feel the heat on your skin. The wind in your hair. The pyramids in front of you. Then visualize yourself becoming lucid in your dream. You can even include a chosen reality check in your visualization process. Maintain your visualization for as long as you can. Doing this helps to increase your chances of becoming lucid in the dream! You're training your mind to have the experience before you sleep.

Simply repeat this process until you fall asleep. As with regular dream incubation, persist until you successfully incubate your lucid dream. Most importantly, remember that this can very easily be a joyful experience if you approach it with lightheartedness and appreciation!

Once you become lucid in your dream there are no limits to what you can explore in the dreamscape. You could for example walk through the pyramids, fly above them, and even speak to the people around there. It's also helpful to note that you can experience one place as many times as you want to. For example: you could request that you go to Egypt in the 1920s. The possibilities are as limitless as your imagination. Then if you really want to have a severe "aha" moment, wake up and research what you dreamed about. For example, if you saw a specific hieroglyph or a specific monument or image, google it and see if your dream was accurate in its imagery. You may very well be surprised!

SHAPE-SHIFTING IN YOUR LUCID DREAMS

If you use your lucid dreaming as a practice to go beyond your perceived identity of separation, you will discover something incredible. You will experience yourself in relation to your nonphysical essence. You may even begin to question your beliefs and assumptions about identity and reality when you wake up.

In a lucid dream you can also morph into something other than you.

You can shape-shift. You can dream yourself into becoming a bird, a plant, or even a different gender or race. Shamans will tell you that you can shape-shift in your waking life too. And I would agree. Although, sadly, I have yet to morph into a cat in my waking life! If shape-shifting into an animal (in either reality) is too far a leap for you, then perhaps think about it in this way:

When you go from illness to wellness, what's happened? You've moved from one state of being to another. You have shape-shifted. You have transformed your energy. You have alchemized illness to wellness. What happens when you age? Your body shape-shifts from one form into another. In a lucid dream you do this shape-shifting consciously, not through your body's automatic and biological processes. You shape-shift with your "lucid dream" body and this can happen in an instant.

This is what shape-shifting can feel like in a lucid dream:

I'm awake in my dream. After I clear out the dreamscape through removing any psychological projections, I will myself to become a river. In that moment I am connected to water. I am the water and the realism of the feeling is very difficult to explain. I am overwhelmed by a flood of oneness. The sense of life that pulsates through the water and the sheer emotion wakes me up.

Here's another experience from Ben,* a dream retreat participant of mine:

"I am lucid in my dream; I do the practices in order to stabilize the dream, trying to remain calm the entire time. It works this time because I don't wake up (a new victory for me). Then I shout, 'I am a lion.' With that I change into a lion. I feel the sentience of what it means to be this animal. Words cannot explain the enormity of the experience. I wake up from my lucid dream completely emotional! I was so moved by my experience of what it means to be a lion that I decided to make a monthly contribution to Panthera.org, a wildlife-oriented nonprofit that saves big cats worldwide."

When you lucid dream with the intention of unity, experience, and humility you come to see your place in the net of life, as well as the place of all other beings and creatures. It's very hard to walk away from a pivotal lucid dream experience without feeling like your waking life has changed in some way. That you have shifted in some way, knowing that you have the power to alter life both through deliberate dreaming and action taking.

The more proficient that you become in your dream practice, the easier it becomes to leap into the void of the unknown. In doing so, you allow yourself to experience more of the larger picture with less judgment and separation. When you shape-shift in a lucid dream, you learn to be the essence of that very thing as opposed to experiencing that thing (or animal or element) as outside of you.

If you let them, judgment and a limited perception of the world (and dreams) will get in the way of your development, by dismissing experiences as beyond the realm of "normal." With all dream work you have to trust yourself enough to experience things firsthand, and you need to be open enough to explore wholeheartedly, without any preconceived notions of what it should feel like.

PRACTICAL EXERCISE: RELEASING CONTROL OF THE OUTCOME IN YOUR LUCID DREAMS

It may seem counterintuitive to learn how to lucid dream only to then willingly relinquish total control of what you do in the dream. But this is more of an intuitive approach to lucid dreaming, one in which you allow yourself to be directly shaped by the dream itself. You experience the lucid dream partially as an observer and partially as an active participant.

The process of going inward is in many ways a paradoxical act of letting go of control in order to become more self-actualized. You don't finalize or excessively control what you are going to experience in the dream. Rather, you allow the dream to take you on the journey you need. You may want to experience lucid dreaming in this way and see what comes up for you. Ultimately, we think we have to control everything. Yet when we stop trying to control the outcome, we find ourselves in the release of control, and through that we experience our intuition and receptive sense of self.

AN EXERCISE IN SURRENDER:
SHOW ME WHAT I NEED TO KNOW

Step 1: Set the intention that you will be safe, protected, and at ease during your lucid dream. One in which you will be shown what you need to know.

Step 2: When you become lucid in the dream, stabilize the dream if need be, and then begin to explore what you are seeing in the dreamscape. You can even pose the question, "Show me what I need to know?" to the dreamscape.

Step 3: Then travel through your dream as if you were a tourist in a foreign country. See where the dream road leads you. Know at all times you can wake yourself up or alter the dream entirely should you want to. You can close your eyes in a lucid dream if you are feeling very overwhelmed and that will usually do the trick in waking you up. Or just shout "Wake up!"

Step 4: Interact with dream elements as they organically appear in the dream. Ask open-ended questions and listen to the answers.

Step 5: Wake up when you are ready to. Write down your lucid dream experience.

Step 6: If you feel the need move on to interpreting your lucid dream experience, ask yourself the following questions: First, how can this dream help me to balance my physical and spiritual life? Second, what psychological and intuitive insight can aid me here? And finally, is there any way I can use my dream to improve my life, or the lives of others, through taking deliberate action? If so, what is the next right step? If you need more guidance, sleep on it.

CHAPTER 10

MANIFESTING IN YOUR WAKING LIFE WITH THE POWER OF YOUR LUCID DREAMS

The work of inspirational speaker and author Esther Hicks (often credited as Abraham-Hicks) offers a foundational explanation for the nature of reality that in turn influences dreaming. In essence, as their message goes: we all have the power to co-create our waking lives, with the Universe (or Non-Physical), through managing our vibration. That means that our thoughts have power. Our emotions and thoughts together affect our energy. Our energy is then responsible for our vibration. Our vibration then brings to us—or rather, we become an energetic match for—the types of experiences (the good, the bad, and the ugly) that we have.

According to Abraham-Hicks, you are either in vibrational align-ment with well-being and the things you want to experience, or you are in resistance to them. It is that simple. Sort out your vibration and your experiences will begin to change too. This is the basis of what many contemporary New Age teachers use to describe the "law of at-traction," or the ability to manifest in waking life. I don't believe the dynamics of creating in life are so one-dimensional but I have found that lucid dreaming can positively influence the speed with which you can manifest experiences in your waking life. And I do believe it is be-cause of an energetic shift in vibration—exactly like what Abraham-Hicks talks about.

This belief is actually not a new one, it is an ancient one. Animists believe they can change the world through energy shifts (they also be-lieve that everything has a life force or energetic pulse and should be treated with respect, which I wholeheartedly agree with). Shamans often used lucid dreaming in order to influence the waking world—although they likely did not use the word "manifesting." The Jewish mystical text, the Zohar, also speaks to the dynamic notion of influ-ence between the seen and the unseen.

As you've seen, the more proficient you become as a lucid dreamer the easier it becomes for you to create very specific experiences in the dreamscape. You can try experiences on, so to speak. And as you've seen through the dreams of healing, shifting things in a dreamscape can influence your waking life.

In Abraham-Hicks lingo we could say that when you are in a lucid dream you change your vibration. Now here's the thing: if on waking you can maintain that specific vibration, then you can become a beacon for the experiences you are hoping to have.

For example, say that you have the desire to be a homeowner but have yet to be able to become one. You could specifically incubate a lucid dream with the intention of buying a house. In your lucid dream you would come to know the feeling of buying your first home. The main goal of your lucid dream would simply be to feel the exhilaration of what it actually feels like to buy that house.

On waking you could then more accurately tap into the feeling (and its vibration) that would then help you to get into alignment with it. Meaning that you could co-create a situation in which you buy a house faster in reality.

You can practice manifesting anything that you want in your lucid dreams. You practice for two reasons. The first is so that you can see if any spontaneous dream symbols pop up in the process. If they do, it usually means that you are being shown what is actually helping you achieve or hindering you from achieving your goal in your waking life. Much like an unconscious belief or habit of self-sabotage that's getting in the way. (There's a practical exercise at the end of this chapter explaining this in more depth.)

The second reason as to why you would actually want to practice manifesting in your lucid dreams is because you can come to know the vibrational essence of it more closely. Once you feel you know the essence of it, you can then *be* that vibration in your waking life. Much like shape-shifting into a lion in a lucid dream. For all intents and purposes you are the essence of it for that time period.

As Abraham-Hicks show:

We become an energetic match, through our vibration, for the types of experiences (the dream-worthy ones and the not-so-great ones) that we have. Once again, you are either in vibrational alignment with what you want or you are in resistance to it. It is that simple. Sort out your vibration and the things you want to experience have to make their way to you.

So why don't more people know about this? Well, here's the thing: lucid dreaming, up until relatively recently (I'm talking the late '90s), wasn't very popular especially in the West.

So who had the keys to this golden and secret dream club before then? Ancient religions and schools of spirituality such as Hinduism, shamanism, and Buddhism, which generally only passed down this knowledge through oral traditions of wisdom-keeping and sharing. So if you weren't part of a lineage in which this ancient sharing of knowledge was offered, it's unlikely that you would have heard about it.

THE GOLDEN KEY TO A SECRET DREAM CLUB

In a radical move, Bön Buddhist Tenzin Wangyal Rinpoche decided to share his knowledge of how to lucid dream with the West. He did so in 1998 with the release of his book *The Tibetan Yogas of Dream and Sleep*. Prior to that point, Eastern practices of lucid dreaming were predominantly kept secret (even in the East). This is what he said in his book as to why this dream wisdom was not previously shared openly:

"The teachings were traditionally maintained as secret teachings, both as a sign of respect and as a protection against dilution through the misunderstanding of unprepared practitioners. They were never taught publicly nor given lightly, but were reserved for individuals who had prepared to receive them."

In his book he explained that he made the decision to share this wisdom because he felt that conditions in the world had changed and that it was necessary to try something new. We could say that he took a great leap of faith, for the collective good, by openly sharing this previously safeguarded wisdom with the world.

The knowledge of how to lucid dream, throughout history, usually has been reserved solely for the healers, medicine women, holy people, or the shamans of the communities. (Or what analyst Toni Wolff called the medial woman.) That is, people gifted with the natural ability to have one foot in the nonphysical world, and one in the physical world, at the same time.

Yet, I believe that we all have this ability. After all, don't we all dream? Most of us have simply forgotten how to perceive spirit because of the way we were raised. We are conditioned into shutting off receptivity to spirit because it doesn't neatly fit in with what we are taught to believe. Many of us come to believe that we can only access spirit through something external to ourselves. Dreaming proves otherwise.

Dreaming is universal. It doesn't matter how much money you have, your gender, your ethnicity, or your relationship status—dreaming is intrinsic and access to it isn't based on any external condition. We all connect to spirit each and every night when we dream. Dreaming is one of the most direct and individualized pathways to remembering that we are all connected in this way. So no matter your title: Whether you are a medicine woman or lawyer, when you dream you are simply your nonphysical essence. Lucid dreaming is for us all and so is creating a life that feels good to live!

PRACTICAL EXERCISE: I KNOW MY DREAM IS ON THE WAY

In this exercise, I'm going to show you exactly how to dream with deliberate intention, so that you can attempt to manifest positive experiences in your life. Before we get started there are two key factors that you need to know about. First, many ancient dream practices maintain that there are karmic consequences for altering the dream world. So it is wise to practice with a level of high integrity and good ethics. If you wouldn't do something in front of someone you love and respect, then don't do it in the dream world.

Second, according to Abraham-Hicks and pretty much any other spiritual belief system, Non-Physical or spirit, is a form of pure loving or positive energy. When you lucid dream you dream with spirit *and your psyche.*

So if anything pops up in your dream that feels other than pure loving energy, then it is important that you are discerning with what you are interacting with. Most of the time, it is simply an external representation of something that is going on within you. A symbolic projection of sorts that comes from within your very own psyche. Meaning that your ego and emotions have gotten in the way of the connection to perceive spirit clearly. Much like with what happens in regular dreaming.

I've have had many lucid dreams wherein my emotions or thoughts have influenced the dreamscape, and as you've seen through the first half of this book, your emotions, memories, and experiences can and will influence your dreams. Quite frankly, sometimes facing emotions or repressed memories, or underlying beliefs unexpectedly (or expectedly), in a lucid dream can be startling!

For example, I once had a lucid dream in which I stabilized the dream, told all my projections to begone, and then was preparing to practice deliberate dreaming with the intention of manifesting something in my life. The experience was going great when all of a sudden the floor caved in and I fell through! Remember, it all feels very real.

I was so blindsided by the shift in the dreamscape that I woke up. The floor caving in was very symbolic for me—the foundation I was building on in my life was weak. I needed to strengthen my belief in myself and what I was creating. The floor caving in also didn't feel like pure loving energy. Rather, it was a symbol from my psyche.

Usually unexpected dream symbols (people or experiences, for example) tend to mimic the intrapsychic energy attributed to the emotion, belief, or unconscious pattern. So they "get you" with evocative and intense imagery! For example, if you've been repressing something for years (so much so that it's getting in the way of your manifesting or creating what you do want in your waking life) then the dream symbols you see, which represent that repression, will very likely be incredibly charged.

Perhaps you want to manifest a house but at the same time you have an internal association to what a home means that carries a negative emotional charge for you. Maybe your childhood home was volatile and transient. You would need to first face the emotion that you have been avoiding so that you can move forward unencumbered. In a way, you might need to spring-clean your psyche's home before you can manifest a beautiful home in your waking life. You can do this spring-cleaning in your waking life and in your lucid dreams!

Again, anything that has a strong emotional charge for you will likely be represented as a strong and commanding symbol in your dream. The dream symbol will be overwhelming in nature either by the sheer look and experience of it or it will be diminutive, which makes you recognize it because it feels out of place, something that, by its pure essence, commands you to pay attention to it. These kinds of symbols are usually extreme because the energy we build around them is extreme. As such they carry momentum even in our sleep.

This sort of thing has happened to almost all the dreamers I know and isn't cause for concern. It just means that when you lucid dream you need to be cognizant of the fact that it is highly likely that you will meet your own emotions, thoughts, unconscious motivators, and drives face-to-face in a dream—the very things that influence your energetic vibration.

These could appear in the form of a dream figure, landscape, or symbol. Sometimes the experience of it is easy and other times it's a bit more intense. It will all depend on your personal history and life experiences and what you are currently trying to manifest in your life.

Remember that *dreams adapt to the dreamer*—this is crucial to remember. Your dreams will adapt to you! Your dream will show you exactly what you need to see so that you can be guided forward positively, if that is your intention. This is especially so if you are trying to manifest something in your waking life.

If an emotion is so strong, or a thought so influential, that it carries through into a dream, then from a psychological standpoint it is definitely worth spending the time investigating what it means in your waking life. You do this so that you can unburden yourself of any emotional baggage in order to feel better.

Once again, as a gentle reminder: lucid dreaming is a balancing act between the physical and nonphysical. So if you see something in your lucid dream that is a bit startling, there are three things you can do:

The first is that you can just change the dreamscape: you communicate your will for the dreamscape to change and the dream will change. The second is that you can wake yourself up. The third is that you can brave facing the dream figure or symbol. You can ask it what it wants to tell you in relation to what you are trying to accomplish.

As mentioned earlier, say that you want to become a homeowner and you successfully manage to incubate a lucid dream in order to experience that precise manifestation. So you find yourself in the dream, standing outside on the lawn in front of your new house, the realtor is there about to hand you the keys, when all of a sudden a ferocious, oversize, rabid dog appears out of nowhere. The dog barks at you, ferociously showing its teeth the entire time! (If you don't wake up at this point then you should remind yourself to stay lucid.)

The dog in this instance was not part of what you were deliberately intending to experience. You wanted to experience how good it would feel to buy that house! The dog is a spontaneous symbol that has appeared out of nowhere in the dreamscape. Generally, obstructions or intrusions in a dreamscape mean you are experiencing a projection of something from your psyche. That is, your thoughts, emotions, and memories (both conscious and unconscious) that are influencing what you are trying to manifest.

At this point in the dream you can choose to interact with the dream symbol, or you could simply tell it "Begone!" Either way, in that moment in your dream you have the choice to react to the dog. You could shout at it. You could tell it that it needs to stop and listen to you. You could say "Stop!" in a booming and commanding voice, like you would in your waking life if a dog came at you. Then you could ask the dog why it is there.

The answer the dog gives you may be nonsensical or it may be clear and illuminating. If the answer is clear, then you can choose to work with the content that it has offered you through interpreting its meaning on waking.

The crazy dog is likely a projected representation of your own anger (emotional pain) or a hidden fear associated with becoming a home-owner. Either way, the dog is actually a helpful dream figure and is nothing to be afraid of, even though in the dream it may feel otherwise. If you get an answer that is helpful, you should thank the dog and send it on its merry way.

The dog is a symbol of something that comes from within you; it is not a clear reflection of spirit because it does not feel like pure, positive energy. Spirit is pure, loving energy and will be experienced as such.

The dog does not *feel* like pure, positive energy so it shows you that it is a representation from something within your mind.

The goal of any lucid dream that is focused on making something manifest is to see the dream through to completion. This may mean that you walk through your new house once the dog disappears, all the while exploring how it feels to know that that place is now *your* home.

There are no limits as to how many times you can do this exercise. You can incubate as many lucid dreams as you need to see through your manifestation in both your dream life and your waking life.

PRACTICAL STEPS: HOW TO DREAM WITH INTENTION

The process of incubating a lucid dream with the goal of manifesting something in your waking life faster is really a process of going inward and trusting spirit at the same time.

Step 1: During your day, set the intention that you will become lucid in your dream with the goal of experiencing what it would feel like to manifest (enter your goal here). Repeat your intention as often as you can throughout the course of the day. You can set a reminder on your cell for your intention to pop up on the hour, every hour.

Step 2: When you are ready and are in bed, set another intention that you will be safe, protected, and at ease during your lucid dream.

Step 3: Use one of the techniques that I outlined in chapter eight on how to become lucid in your dreams. Such as the DILD (dream induced lucid dream) method. Remember that the key factor to becoming lucid in your dreams lies in your ability to recognize the dream for a dream!

Step 4: When you become lucid in your dream, move on to stabilizing the dream. Then declare out loud what you are trying to deliberately manifest to the dreamscape. You could say: "Dream, I would like to experience buying my dream home now!" Or "Dream, I would like to experience what it would feel like to be working in a great job!"

Step 5: The goal of this exercise is to experience the vibration of the goal you are trying to manifest. That is so that you can carry through that vibration in your waking life so that you may see it happen.

Step 6: Use your judgment to interact wisely with any spontaneous dream symbols (like people or animals) that may pop up in the dream.

Step 7: Try and remain lucid throughout the dream to see your manifestation completed.

Step 8: Once that is done you should wake yourself up from the dream. At this point I recommend that you get out of bed and write down, or voice note, your experience so that you solidify what the experience felt like. The core goal is to remember the feeling state!

Step 9: Repeat the entire exercise as often as you see fit.

CHAPTER 11

SOUL GUIDED

I n depth psychology, the liminal space between the unconscious and conscious facets of one's psyche are mediated through a psychopomp. The word itself is rooted in the Greek word ψυχοπομπός ("psyche" and "pompos"), and is translated as Soul Guide or Guide of the Soul. Through mythology we come to learn of the psychopomp's important role in assisting a central figure's transition from one state of being to another. Through dreaming we come to meet the Soul Guide.

The psychopomp is recognized as a guide (symbolically it can be an animal, or a wise old man, or woman) that helps the person during a transition, usually from death to the afterlife. However, the transition isn't strictly about death and the afterlife. It can be any form of transition that simply requires crossing a threshold.

Moving through adulthood into midlife, or going from being single to being married, are common transitions. Many people cross the threshold of being single through the symbolic ritual of marriage and a wedding. Once the rites have been spoken the couple cross the threshold and are wed. The old way of being has "died" (each is no longer single) and the new way of being has been "born" (they are married).

Yet, before we cross any threshold there is usually a liminal space where what was and what will be hangs in the balance. A time when we have to embrace the in-between. For example, the liminal time of pregnancy when one is preparing for the crossover from womanhood into motherhood. (Pregnancy dreams are often vivid, intense, and helpful as they guide all women during this pivotal process of transformation.)

We experience transitioning, liminal spaces, and the psychopomp in many ways with dreamwork. On a pragmatic level we even cross the liminal threshold between waking and sleeping in order to enter into dreaming. If you have explored the hypnagogic and hypnopompic states (chapter seven can offer you a refresher), you will have noticed that that liminal passage of transition between waking consciousness and sleep consciousness is rich with images and figures.

Liminal spaces are not empty no-man's-lands. They are the places of the in-between. Liminal spaces are the connectors, just as bridges, passageways, or even portals embrace the in-between space of "all that was" and "all that will be." If you pay attention to your dreams during liminal spaces in your own life, you will come to see that a Soul Guide is likely present in them.

As you've seen over the course of this book, both your regular dreams and lucid dreams link you to spirit. In regular dreams, a Soul Guide is often recognized symbolically. In a lucid dream, conscious interaction with a Soul Guide can be had.

Take the following regular dream as an example:

A woman has the following dream shortly after the death of her mother. In the dream she is with her daughter and they are traveling, but to an unknown destination. She knows the destination is important and has something to do with their new home, but the dream feels ambiguous. All of a sudden, as dreams are, they find themselves standing outside a train terminal. She wants her daughter to get on the train with her. But instead her daughter tells her that she wants to get on another train with her grandmother (who has not appeared in the dream) and that she'll return to her shortly.

On waking, this woman felt saddened by her dream, as is so often the case when we dream of someone who has just passed away. Yet what lingered with her was the concern that her daughter went with her mother instead of her. What did that mean?

The daughter in her dream symbolically has a dual function: as a reflection of the mother's own inner child and as a Soul Guide/psychopomp for the grandmother.

Through reflection the dreamer came to realize that the death of her parent made her feel like she was no longer someone's child. The dream narrates and acknowledges her loss and grief palpably. It also speaks to her transition from being an adult child to simply being a parent, a journey she goes through alone.

In the dream, the young daughter gets on the train to journey with the grandmother to an unknown destination (the afterlife), while the mother gets on a train to go to a new home. Here we symbolically see the young child's choice to be the Soul Guide for the grandmother. On reflection this dream greatly consoled the dreamer. It acknowledged and validated her grief, as well as her visceral loss. Yet at the same time, it showed her that all three women of the lineage were transitioning, each in her own way, together. How beautiful.

LUCID DREAMS AND GUIDES

In a lucid dream we interact with the psychopomp in two different ways. The first is that as lucid dreamers we can meet with people who have passed on and assist them if need be. In doing so, we act as the psychopomp figure. For example, if a late loved one has a message they'd like to send to a living family member, a skilled lucid dreamer can receive it and pass it on. We can personally be guided during any liminal transition that we are experiencing, simply through requesting a meeting with a guide in our lucid dreams. It is a bidirectional relationship when working within lucid dreams.

Again, transitioning isn't always about death. It can be about any meaningful evolution or change, like transitioning from being an employee to starting your own business, or going from working life to retirement. It's simply a period of change that requires the ending of an identity, or a completion of an old way of doing something. I've chosen to use examples with deceased dream figures simply to show you the weight that these times carry. To show you how supported we are through our dreams, and how we can either be the receiver of emotional support or the provider, depending on the circumstances.

Here is a lucid dream example from the prolific personal development author and speaker Dr. Wayne Dyer, who received emotional comfort through his lucid dream. He had this dream shortly after his mother passed away and found great closure and happiness from it:

In the dream he is driving up the road to his mother's house. Then, as dreams are, he is suddenly at the front door, only to notice that it is covered by a screen door. In that moment he realizes the screen door is out of place. His mother's house does not have a screen door! This recognition triggers a lucid dream.

Now lucid in the dream, he attempts to open the screen door. He tries and tries to open the door but to no avail. Then his mother, who looks like a forty-year-old version of herself, simply appears and opens the door inward. All of this surprises him as he recollects that his mother has recently passed away. (Remember, in a lucid dream you still have access to all of your lived experiences and memories!)

In disbelief he exclaims, "You can't be here because you're dead!" And in that moment she fades away. Seconds later she reappears in the dream. Only this time, she appears as the ninety-six-year-old version of the woman that she had been before she passed on. Flooded with emotion, he wakes up.

I love the story of Wayne Dyer's lucid dream experience and I shared it with you because it so aptly shows the dance between the physical and nonphysical.

Just as Wayne Dyer experienced, you too will experience the influence of your thoughts, emotions, and memories in your lucid dreams. All of us do. That is, until we are all more proficient in our dream practice.

In his dream, he cried out that his mother was dead! If she was dead, how could she be there? His conscious mind questioned her presence. At this point she disappeared. His thoughts and emotions influenced the lucid dream through his questioning. Then she suddenly reappeared as an older version of herself. That is a version he was more familiar with!

Imagine if you had just had a *spontaneous* lucid dream in which you saw a passed loved one. It can be overwhelming to just think of someone who has passed, never mind actually seeing them in a dream in which you are conscious!

Part of the art of perceiving spirit is accepting the experience simply for what it is: different from the physical. Wayne Dyer went on to ask Abraham-Hicks (in a recorded video conversation available online) why his mother couldn't stay longer with him in the dream. The answer to his question wasn't that she couldn't remain with him. **It was that he couldn't perceive her anymore.**

This makes a lot of sense to me. His emotions influenced his ability to perceive her. It's likely also why he woke up involuntarily in the dream—his emotions flooded him. So to drive my point home: in a lucid dream you are able to perceive spirit but your thoughts and emotions can cloud that connection.

This is one of the reasons why I offered mindfulness practices in this book: so that you can experience spirit more clearly. They also can help you to feel better all around in your waking life. A double bonus!

So how do you know if a lucid dream figure is really a deceased loved one or spiritual guide? You ask them for evidence. Most dream guides will offer you information that can then be "fact-checked" on waking. You can also alter the lucid dreamscape by once again saying, "All projections begone!" Equally, the more you explore your own dreams, the more you will come to trust your own inner wisdom and knowing.

As a writer it can be curious to weigh down ethereal concepts with words because it's antithetical to the actual experience and essence of them. If you've ever experienced your intuition profoundly you'll know exactly what I mean. If I asked you to "prove" your intuition to me, right now in this moment, could you?

You'd know that intuition, like lucid dreaming, is a beautiful and mysterious dance between the physical and nonphysical. Between the seen and the unseen. Defining that dance is like trying to hold on to the wind. Rather, it's something that you feel, like the wind—on your face.

This sentiment resonates with what mystical texts say about dreaming too. You experience it. You embody it. You are it. You muse about it. Yet it still remains a mystery. Dreaming, like intuition, is a form of wisdom that goes beyond logic. It is a way of perceiving nonphysical with conscious awareness.

Through lucid dreaming we also come to learn that time, in a linear sense, seems totally inadequate as an explanation of conscious experience. There is a divine matrix of wisdom and creation unfathomable to the logical mind that takes us into the realm of infinite possibilities; past, present, and future lives; and the ability to create more intentionally together with spirit in our waking lives.

Dreaming isn't a one-dimensional experience reduced to clinical or critical thinking. Dreaming is an art. There are so many layers and levels to it, of which this book has just scratched the surface.

In lucid dreams we take our awareness and memory (egoic self) with us into the dreamscape. This is can be beneficial and helpful, but it can also cloud our connection to spirit.

This is exactly what happened in the dream experience of Wayne Dyer when he recognized his mother as being too young in the dream. And so his mother reappeared in his lucid dream as the age she was prior to passing. In his dream, she changed into a ninety-six-year-old woman—a more "accurate" image for his rational mind to process as real.

It's also worth noting once again that this was his first spontaneous lucid dream experience. So we wouldn't expect him to be in total control of his focus and awareness at that point in a dream; but it does teach us the importance of using our attention properly.

Dr. Dyer's lucid dream also shows us that regardless of how skilled one is as a lucid dreamer, spirit adapts to what we are experiencing to help us maintain our connection—*to communicate with us, no matter where we are on our journey.* No matter how much our mind, emotions, and memories get in the way.

Nevertheless, I often get asked why dreamers don't dream in one specific way in relation to spirit. For example, why doesn't everyone dream of one type of spiritual guide? Or why don't all the family members dream of the same person who has just passed away? To which my answer is usually the same:

We are individuals who are at different points in our journey with completely different belief systems and life experiences. It wouldn't make sense for all of us to get the same message in the same way, because we don't all need the same thing, at the same time, from spirit. Not everyone needs closure with a late loved one.

Dreams are so special in the sense that they take the base of our personal physical experiences and mix them with our nonphysical essence, to give us greater insight and guidance for what we need to know. Dreams speak to us about gaining a higher perspective. Ultimately, your dreams are guiding you, so that you may rise and experience your life from a greater vantage point.

DREAM GUIDES CAN TAKE MANY FORMS

Anna* joined me during one of my dream retreats and provided a wonderful example of how spirit will connect with us when we are ready, and in a way that makes us pay attention. For the most part, Anna identified as a semi-atheist, who didn't really know if any of this dream stuff or intuitive stuff was real, but a few very powerful lucid dreams had shaken her to her core. So she decided to venture out and try something new, and as a result there she was—sleeping over—at a retreat with other dreamers.

She announced that her intention for the retreat was to give spirit a chance to prove to her that she should listen. In the same breath she said that she didn't think her "guide" could be a person. Remember how I've said our words have power? Well, Anna packed quite a punch with that intention. The retreat proceeded with participants experiencing the most incredible dreams, overcoming unconscious beliefs and triggers, and at the same time deepening their own connection to spirit.

Yet, she felt as though nothing really happened—even though she incubated her regular dreams with the intention of meeting her spiritual guide. Night after night she told me that she simply dreamed that she was in different situations and on three occasions a dog appeared to her in her dreams. I asked her what kind of dog it was and she told me that it was a border collie (aka a sheepdog). Anna thought the dog symbolized something that was simply coming from within her psyche. And as you've seen over the course of this book, of course she could have been correct because we dream with our psyches in tandem with spirit.

I met Anna at the level of her dream symbolism. What does a sheepdog mean to you? "Sheepdogs are herders. They're loyal and they never leave their flock," she said. Ironically, her dream had a scriptural sound to it. So there is a loyal guide dog that will never leave you? Hmm, interesting! What do sheep, as symbols, represent to you? "The inability to think for myself, and it speaks to behaving sheepishly," she replied.

Anna's fear was that she would lose her intellectual edge through connecting with the more inexplicable aspects of life. That she would be left out of or ridiculed by her community for believing in a spiritual aspect to life. Her dream spelled it all out for her. She was guided. Her guide was loyal to her no matter what her beliefs were.

Anna chose to do some contemplative reflection to really look at some of the beliefs she was holding on to. She decided to make some fundamental changes and began to more boldly express what really resonated with her. About a month after the retreat, I received an e-mail from Anna. She had had a powerful lucid dream wherein she requested to meet her guide. A woman appeared to her in the dreamscape and told her that she had also "sent" Anna the border collie dream.

Spirit will adapt to you and the unique process that you are going through. You don't need to control this process—you simply need to meet your guides halfway. Ultimately, our dream guides are there to help us: to show us that we are never truly alone.

CONNECTING WITH YOUR OWN DREAM GUIDES AND THE ART OF SYNCHRONICTY

People who attend my dream workshops often come with the intention of establishing a connection with their own dream guide (or spiritual guide, if you prefer). Sometimes participants meet more than one guide. You may also come to find that you meet more than one guide, so simply remain open to the process that presents itself to you. As with Anna, the process is what counts.

As you've seen over the course of this book, we can experience spirit in many ways, both in our waking life and our dream life. You can hold the intention to meet your guide either in your waking life or through your dreams. Equally, if you have yet to experience the wonder that is lucid dreaming, that does not need to be a barrier to meeting your guide. Simply use your deliberate intention to open the doors of communication with spirit.

So how exactly does spirit communicate with you, me, and everyone else in our waking lives? Through any means necessary! But mostly through intuitive hints, signs, symbols, and meaningful coincidence. For example, when you read a social media post with relevant and helpful words at exactly the right time for you. Or when you walk into a store and hear a song that offers meaningful, comforting, and helpful lyrics for a problem that you are facing—again, at just the right time. Or when you randomly walk past two strangers and hear them talking about a topic that is relevant to you too. These are all examples of the ways in which spirit is clamoring to get your attention.

It has also been my experience that spirit communicates with us in a manner that we find most comfortable to accept in our waking lives. I am most comfortable receiving guidance audibly (clairaudience) through my dreams and via my intuition. Maybe you are the same? Or maybe you would like to develop your own receptive abilities further, so that you can have a deeper, more active relationship with spirit and receive the guidance meant uniquely and specifically for you.

For the most part, it tends to take a lot of repetition for most people to accept that the messages they are receiving (in their waking lives) from spirit *are real*. That is why synchronicity, meaningful repetition, and coincidence feels so wonderful—because it "wakes us up" to what spirit is telling (or showing) us. It often provides us with much-needed external validation of inner knowing.

We often make spirit work very hard to get our attention! We need big, bold messages so obvious in nature, but totally unanticipated, to believe that we are being communicated with. I've found this especially in the West. Most people are taught to dismiss spirit at an early age, so as quickly as they receive messages, they are just as quick to dismiss them.

So the first step in connecting is to decide to actually just be in an active relationship with spirit. Perhaps you've already done this, or deepened this relationship, simply through reading this book? The second step is to use your deliberate intention. Before you go to bed, request that you meet your spirit guide in your regular dreams. Maintain your nightly presleep intention until you feel this has occurred.

If you feel that you need a slight refresher on how to incubate your regular dreams, then simply page back to the end of chapter two, exercise #1, where I outlined exactly how to do this. Remember, like Anna, you may have a dream that you feel is nothing special or important but in actuality is deeply moving and therefore worthy of your attention. Try to keep an open mind and heart when you explore the connection to your guides.

If you can lucid dream, then simply clear the dreamscape as well as any psychological projections and request a meeting with your guide. Again, this is a bidirectional relationship, so act like you would if you were meeting someone important in your waking life. Don't place any irrational demands on your guide, although you can of course ask your guide for additional information (or signs) and request assistance with whatever you are struggling with. My experience is that life then becomes incredibly fun with synchronous moments happening when you least expect them!

MEETING OTHER LUCID DREAMERS IN THE DREAMSCAPE

When I was researching stories of other lucid dreamers for this book, I stumbled upon a wonderful panel discussion hosted by the SAND (Science and Non-Duality) symposium. In the symposium, artist and professor Fariba Bogzaran, PhD, shared one of her incredible lucid dream experiences. Bogzaran's core intention for all of her lucid dreams was simply to meet with the omniscient part of herself and God. She held this intention for more than two and a half years!

During that time she had many lucid dreams in which she met with a Tibetan Buddhist lama who taught her how to deepen her own lucid dream practice. As many people would assume, Professor Bogzaran thought that the Buddhist lama in her lucid dreams was simply a meaningful projection of her own psyche or an ethereal spirit guide. But here's the kicker: twelve years later she met Lama Garchen Rinpoche in her waking life and they both recognized each other from the lucid dream space.

He was the very same Buddhist lama from her dreams, and had been teaching her the entire time! As a result of their synchronous meeting, she then went on to train with him for over a decade in both her waking life and dream life.

Bogzaran's dream experience also highlights why we should ask for clarity as to who we are speaking to in a lucid dream. It's a vast and expansive dreamscape with many dreamers in it, so it's helpful to request clarity right from the get-go!

As you've come to see, the lucid dream experience is so much more than just a psychological projection of the mind. The dream world is the space (or place) where our nonphysical essence meets with the rest of Non-Physical (spirit). In that experience we can meet fellow lucid dreamers, spiritual guides, and even departed loved ones. All of whom we can learn from and speak to.

You will see that adventures of all kinds will happen to you as you become more proficient in your own lucid dream practice. You'll also learn to tell the difference between your psychological projections and dream beings as you practice both your regular dream work and your lucid dream work.

Remember, if you are in doubt in a lucid dream you can simply say

"All thought-forms disappear!" and if you don't feel good about a dream figure, just move along. Your intuition will not steer you wrong. And as always, the underlying intention of the dream (and the words you use) can and will alter the course of your lucid dream practice.

For Professor Bogzaran, her intention was to incubate a dream in order to meet the omniscient. She certainly achieved an element of that. For most Tibetan Bön Buddhists, the core goal of a lucid dream practice is ultimately a transcendental one—that of enlightenment. My current lucid dream intention is (and has been for a while) simply to allow the lucid dream to take me on a journey of wholehearted discovery. *What's yours?*

Finally, if you would like to attempt to meet up with other lucid dreamers in the dreamscape, I invite you to check out my online dream circle where we deliberately dream in a group. I have different groups for non-lucid and lucid dreamers where we set specific intentions or goals together. You can see these on my website (athenalaz.com).

CHAPTER 12

A POWERFUL DREAMER
DREAMS FOR ALL

Waking reality is a shared dream and our shared dream is turning into a collective nightmare. The earth needs us to pay attention to the ways that we create (dream!) on autopilot and we need to embrace our diverse differences in order to experience peace. It's so easy to fall into despair but if all dreamers wake up to the fact that we are actively influencing and co-creating our collective dream—our waking reality—then we can change things through dream visioning and then through taking very aligned waking actions.

Earlier in this book, I took you on a journey of discovering how your personal unconscious beliefs influence your waking life. You saw how your regular nighttime dreams illuminate your unconscious beliefs by showing you specific imagery and dream symbols.

For example, someone who has a desire to be successful but who gets in their own way through, say, self-sabotage or procrastination, will often dream of other people blocking them. The dreamer projects their own unconscious (or shadow) belief onto others and the dream highlights this through the shadow dream figures. The dream forces the dreamer to ask: Why am I always being blocked from reaching my destination? Who is getting in the way? Through mindful, self-reflective questions the dreamer becomes more aware of their interior life—to their own beliefs. They realize their own beliefs of scarcity or past experiences are getting in the way of what they wholeheartedly desire.

We all have the capacity for lower impulses linked to unconscious belief systems. For example, most people can imagine a situation in which violence becomes an option. Don't think that's you? What if someone had a weapon against your child or partner's head? We can easily fall into something without meaning to. That is why it is so important that we all become deliberate dreamers. That we become mindful and awake to the fact that we are co-creating our realities. That we choose deliberately.

As a collective, our unconscious beliefs influence our collective reality. A great way of understanding this concept is through seeing what is being shown in film and the media. Our collective fear is projected out onto the screen. Division, hate, greed, lack of respect and reverence for others and for nature consume our attention. Simply think about social media and the enormity of hate that gets spewed out there because people can hide behind anonymity! We collectively project a lot of emotional garbage onto social media and then some news outlets do a great job maintaining and peddling mass-market fear.

We've also seen how it can be a short skip and a jump from anonymous microaggressions (on-screen) to active and violent aggression (off-screen). Unconscious impulses love to hide behind extremism, or extreme beliefs, which lend themselves to all-or-nothing thinking, for example, "I am *totally correct* and you are *totally wrong.*" If we believe that there is only one way, or one answer and not another, then we've stepped into the realm of an unconscious pull at play. *Surely, we as a collective can dream better than this?* Perhaps we can find the middle ground where wholeness is held in a beautiful balance of honoring all of our differences.

When we feel highly justified in acts of violence or aggression, psychologically speaking we are likely dealing with the repressed impulses of the egoic mind. For example, do you remember when zombie movies became all the rage? Well, zombies as a collective symbol show us what happens when we act from a brain-dead space. When all of life becomes about mindless, insatiable consuming, for all intents and purposes we've debased ourselves into becoming versions of zombies. We become part of the living dead because we forget the luminosity that animates all of life. We forget our own higher power to dream well, with spirit, by using our attention properly.

When we don't apply our intention and will with conscious awareness, we create poorly. We are no longer deliberate dreamers. We all have to take ownership of our own unconscious (and conscious) destructive natures, desires, and wants if we want our collective reality to get better.

If we all do our own part in our communities, the ripple effect will be profound. We see this so beautifully in action when people come together from all over the world to extend help and service beyond themselves. For example when a crowdfunding campaign aimed at helping people in crisis gains massive traction on the internet. Thousands of individuals donate just a small amount and as a result, millions are sent to a place or to people in crisis and trauma. Empathy can move mountains *and so can collective intention.*

We can imagine ourselves energetically connected to one another in a great cosmic web of life. We are connected to the earth, plants, all the people and animals that equally inhabit waking reality. This notion of interconnectedness and interrelatedness is found in almost all ancient religions. A small shift by one individual creates a ripple effect in the web (even if the person has no awareness of it). When the planet suffers, so do we. We are of the earth, made of matter and spirit.

One of the most powerful stories I can gift to you is that of the

Achuar people. I offer their story to illustrate how we as modern people can begin to dream anew. How we can assist one another and the
earth through a shift in consciousness and dream visioning.

The Achuar people have lived in the Amazon rain forest for thousands
of years. They are the custodians of the forest as well as keepers of an
ancient dream culture who, as a community, still plan their days according to the information that they receive in their nighttime dreams. They
wake collectively in the morning and share their dreams, then take
action accordingly—based on the group's dreams.

In the early '80s the elders and shamans of the group began to experience disconcerting dreams and visions of the modern world invad-
ing and destroying the forest. These visions of course came true when
oil companies pillaged the neighboring territories and clear-cutting
began to provide grazing land. As a result, devastating fires continue
to sweep through the Amazon because of deforestation.

In 1995, a call sounded from the shamans of the Achuar, who were
deep in the heart of natural forest, to seek support from the outside
world. A small number of people answered the call. This call wasn't
sounded through the phone or through modern technology—it was a
spiritual call announced through dreams. I believe that the shamans of
the Achuar used their ability to lucid dream, and higher states of consciousness, to send out dream messages to people who were ready to
hear what they had to say.

As Lynne Twist relayed in an online interview, her work in the Amazon began when she could no longer deny that "call." The Achuar people summoned her to the jungle through her dreams. In her nightly dreams she saw a group of people living in a jungle who had reddish orange symbols painted on their faces and adorned headdresses. Night after night she dreamed of the Achuar.

At the time of her dreams, Lynne had no idea who these people were and had no intention of ever traveling to the Amazon. Her primary focus was on her philanthropic work, which was focused on ending world hunger and really had nothing do to with conservation.

When these dreams commenced, she had no idea that she was being contacted by the shamans of the Achuar. Of course, at first, as most modern people do, she simply dismissed the dreams. Perhaps she ate too much spicy pizza, as a skeptical friend of mine would say!

Yet Lynne continued to dream of the people with reddish orange symbols painted on their faces. At first she saw these people only when she dreamed but then she began to see them in her waking life too. As you can imagine, when she started seeing these dream people in her waking life she started to freak out a bit. Who wouldn't? She thought she was hallucinating, or, perhaps worse, was losing her mind.

It was only when her friend John Perkins recognized the people whom she was describing as the Achuar people that they came to realize that they needed to go to the Amazon. Eventually Lynne, her husband, John, and a few other people would travel to meet the Achuar.

That meeting would result in the creation of the Pachamama Alliance, which is and has been, since its inception, largely responsible for saving and conserving massive parts of the Amazonian jungle.

I believe that the Achuar people *need us all* to answer the call. The Amazon needs us now. All of nature needs us right now. We need to pay attention and change our ways. This isn't just a problem in the West, as it is so often defined by people with the intent to pinpoint blame and by doing so abdicate their own eco-responsibility. It is a worldwide issue.

We collectively create our shared reality. We collectively can create a better, more sacred waking reality. We can envision peace, a healthy planet, and more diverse systems of well-being and then take action to create that. Equally, a small group of deliberate dreamers can make an enormous shift because they have learned to use their intention and will properly. Like dream crowdfunding for the collective good!

IT'S TIME TO WAKE THE DREAMERS

I am here to wake the dreamers. Because you are here and reading this, please consider yourself called. Every chapter that you've journeyed through has gotten you to this very point: to remind you that **you are a deliberate dreamer!** So will you dare to dream for the collective good? Will you use your intention and will in a deliberate way and dream of harmony for the collective, as well as for your own personal well-being? Your vision of your life is as big as the dreams you allow. The vision for the planet is as beautiful as we all allow.

When we come into contact with our own higher power we can dream for the entire web of life. We can move beyond zombie consumerism and mindless distraction and live in greater harmony with nature and with life itself. This doesn't mean that we need to camp out in a cave somewhere—we can collectively hold a dream of modernity in balance. It is still possible to follow your most soul-aligned goals while keeping the well-being of the collective in mind. Our dreams are as unlimited as our capacity to imagine something better.

We most certainly do not need to believe in an all-or-nothing situation. I would like to focus my deliberate intention on clean air, healthy water, and an abundance of nature and animals as well as a greater respect for connection and community. Where we focus our attention has an impact. We can all sing our own tunes while collectively aiming for a harmonious melody. Remember, we call on certain realities to ourselves, so our intention is incredibly important. How will you use yours?

LISTEN TO THE DREAMERS

In my dream I am hovering off the ground. You would think that levitation would trigger my lucidity but it does not. I remain unaware that I am dreaming. I float toward two men who, at the same time, are rising up off the floor in a seated meditation pose. I arrive in front of them and as I do they stop moving, balancing comfortably in midair.

They tell me that they like what I've written in my dream book and that I should remember that there is so much more to lucid dreaming than anyone has ever written before. Then they give me this message: In many ways dreaming is still about learning to listen better. They proceed to tell me to wake up so that I can remember my dream and share the message.

I wake up.

The paradox of dreaming is that through its very illusory nature we break free of material illusions. Dreams always speak to the truth of a much larger picture. And so the art of all dream work is in learning to listen better to spirit and your own psyche. If you learn to listen to the guidance of your dreams you will be shown what movement to take in your life. You'll be pointed toward your true north because you are being guided by a source much larger than you.

Ultimately, some things cannot be explained or even known through the intellect. They can only be known through the heart, through the inner world, and through the very same senses that awaken when we sleep. Senses that show us just how thin the perceptual veil is that separates the dreaming world from the physical world. When we dream, we are reminded nightly that we are part of an infinite consciousness.

Most of us are so busy that we don't allow stillness to permeate our beings, but in the process of stillness, like through the journey of dreams, we discover our connection to infinite consciousness.

My dreams amplify this message over and over again:

In the dream I am distracted and searching for something I cannot seem to find. What the "thing" is is unclear to me, but I feel compelled to search. Off I go, searching and searching, but I cannot find what I am seeking. I search under pillows, in drawers, and I even look under the bed. I search the entire house for what feels to be a very long time. Exasperated, I finally surrender, and then I see it. No—I feel—it the sun shining through the windows. Light floods everything and then I wake up.

Aren't we all searching for something that seems to elude us? We toss things over in order to find what we think we need—usually something outside of us.

We get lost in the seeking. When all we need to do is to stop and bask in the luminosity of our inner light.

So, my dear reader, in closing I ask you, isn't that time . . . *now*?

ACKNOWLEDGMENTS

My deepest gratitude to my editor, Sara Carder. Thank you for believing in me and this book. Many thanks to Rachel Ayotte for your detailed care and assistance. To Coleen O'Shea, thank you for your incredible support and guidance throughout this literary adventure. My heartfelt gratitude to Sabila Khan—thank you.

To Victoria Adamo, Alex Casement, Sara Johnson, Anne Kosmoski, Casey Maloney (and the entire team at TarcherPerigee), thank you for being so wonderful!

To all my guides and teachers, thank you for helping me along this journey. To my parents, thank you for all of your love and support. To my incredible husband: You are the light in my life—thank you for your unwavering love and support. To Maria and George, thank you for everything. To Mick and Glenda, my gratitude for your kind encouragement and support. To Keren, thank you for your friendship and honest feedback. Finally, to all the dreamers out there, thank you for believing in the power of your dreams.

INDEX

ABOUT THE AUTHOR

Athena Laz is a counseling psychologist, dream expert, and fourth-generation intuitive. Her online site, www.athenalaz.com, is a global platform that merges spiritual wisdom with psychological know-how. Thousands of people worldwide have enjoyed her courses, membership programs, and retreats. She appears regularly as an expert on TV and has been featured by many multimedia outlets such as *Cosmopolitan*, *Marie Claire*, *Women's Health*, and more.

Also by

ATHENA LAZ

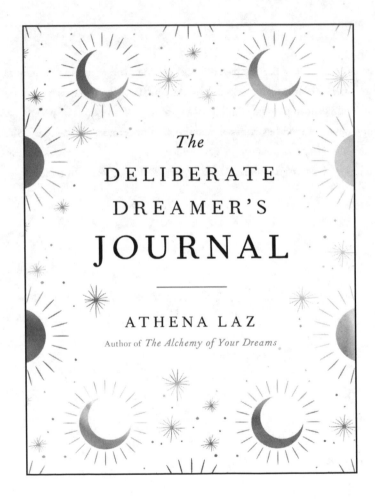

The

DELIBERATE
DREAMER'S
JOURNAL

ATHENA LAZ

Author of *The Alchemy of Your Dreams*

tarcherperigee